Coming Clean

Ending My Affair with Alcohol and
Learning to Be My True Self

By A. Rainy Gibbs

ACKNOWLEDGMENTS

I started writing this book early in my sobriety. I had a desire to put my story on paper. Years after I was sober, I made a new acquaintance, through our dogs, who is an author. We became friends, and I shared what I wrote with her. If it had not been for her encouragement, support, and guidance, this book would not have been published. Thank you, author Kelly McIntire! I also want to thank Cup and Quill Editing and Publishing; Rebecca Stohler who was a wonderful help providing structural editing. And, of course, Jessica Hammerman and her team from Emerald Design Co. for making my book come alive.

A special thank you to my husband, Dan. He stuck by me throughout my addiction and stood by my side always through my recovery and also supported this project. My family on the West Coast showed never-ending support. My niece, Rebecca, who helped me reach my goals with this book and pushed me through some of my fears.

I am blessed to have close friends who watched me walk through this project and believed in me. A special thank you to my sponsor in my recovery program; you are one in a million.

TABLE OF CONTENTS

ACKNOWLEDGMENTS..iii

PROLOGUE vii

INTRODUCTION...1

THE BEGINNING 3

JUNIOR HIGH SCHOOL...11

MY DAD..14

HIGH SCHOOL 16

DIETING AND WEIGHT OBSESSION...............19

THE MOVE 20

POST-HIGH SCHOOL...22

DEPRESSION 29

POST COLLEGE..32

MY FIRST SCHOOL COUNSELOR POSITION 38

MY NEXT CAREER...43

INCREASE OF MY DISEASE...............................50

MOVING ON...54

MARRIAGE 58

RECOGNIZING I NEEDED HELP 61

HITTING MY BOTTOM 68

SURRENDERING 71

HOSPITALIZATION 77

WHEN LIFE THROWS A CURVEBALL 87

NEARING THE END OF MY CAREER 92

THE LOSS OF MY DAD 94

RUFUS..98

WORKING ON ME 100

EPILOGUE...104

PROLOGUE

Hi, my name is Anne, and I am an alcoholic. I found my way into a recovery program and got the nerve to seek a sponsor. The first few words that came out of her mouth were, "I will love you until you can love yourself." I couldn't believe how good that felt, and it brought me to tears. At that point in my life, I did not think I was worth being loved at all! For almost fifteen years, I have had the same sponsor, a woman who has loved me unconditionally every day. My sponsor has guided me through a sober life. That is, I got through difficult times without needing a drink or substance. It means I am a member of a wonderful group of people I found in my recovery group. I also reconnected with the God of my understanding. With all this support, I have remained sober and pray it continues a day at a time.

I am grateful for my husband, family, and close friends. I tried to solve my drinking problem by myself, but as many before me can attest to, it rarely works this way. If I had quit my addictive drinking by myself, I would be what they call, a "dry drunk." This means that I don't drink, yet have the behaviors (isms) of an alcoholic; fear, low self-esteem, self-centeredness, and anger. I would have continued to live like an alcoholic, full of emotional pain and never-ending drama.

INTRODUCTION

I wrote this book to share my experience, strength, and hope. I am certain that others can relate to my experiences with alcohol abuse. I learned to recover by observing great people at my recovery meetings. My life long journey as a recovering alcoholic improves despite life's tragedies. I am grateful that I can say I am a "recovering" alcoholic. I can even say I am proud to be an alcoholic! Weird, huh? Did I ever think I could give up my security blanket, alcohol? No way! But I have achieved fifteen years of sobriety, a day at a time. I accomplished this through hard work and never forgetting my past. I remember the vicious cycle that was my life. It was full of self-doubt, drama, sadness, and anger. I thought that everything was better when I drank. However, the bad feelings were still there the next day, along with the usual hangover.

These days, I live a good life. I am happy, productive, and love myself. Therefore, I can love others! Do I have hard times? Yes, life continues. I can handle it by walking through it with my support system, knowing that I do not have to drink over it. I know that if I take a drink, I might not have another recovery within me. Sobriety enabled me to deal with feelings of anger and hurt I had "stuffed" for years. Now, I enjoy my life. I learned to love my job as a school counselor. I became present in life, and my relationship with my husband improved greatly. I forgave my mom for some of her behaviors toward me as a child. Recovery enabled me to grow closer to her and realize she did and does love me. I learned gratitude toward many things in my life and took responsibility for my actions. I voice my feelings and establish boundaries. This did not happen overnight. It took hard work and support.

Like all addicts, I needed to reach my bottom. For each of us, it happens at different times, and sadly for some, it never happens. For me, and others before me and behind me, there is a life worth living without the use of substances.

If you think there is no way you can ever get sober or clean, please read my story. You might identify with something I went through or said that could help you. If I, who did not think I could put down the drink, so can you. The first step is to realize you have a problem and ask for help. There are many recovery groups out there; you must find the one that works for you. Please realize you cannot do this on your own. You may think you can, but if you are a true alcoholic or addict, you cannot, if you want to lead a healthy and drama-free life. I found the program that worked for me, and it taught me to live a fulfilling, sober life. I grow each day and learn more about myself. I by no means am an expert on addiction; I only have my personal experience. I invite you to read about my life journey and my affair with alcohol.

THE BEGINNING

Living a sober life is huge! There are ups and downs, but that is LIFE. I participate in my life. While I was drinking, I didn't participate. I avoided it. It took me a while to realize this. If I had my life to do over again, I wouldn't change anything. I know that sounds weird, but the things I learned about myself and how to live life as it is meant to be, are so precious to me today. I am grateful I am a recovering alcoholic because I learned a wonderful way to live my life and handle obstacles.

Overall, I had a pleasant childhood. My parents stayed together, we took family vacations, and I had everything I needed as a youngster, teenager, and a young adult. However, there were glitches along the way that shaped my personality. I had low self-esteem, anxiety, fear, and I was a people pleaser. As a young child, I was hypersensitive and wanted to make everyone happy. My dad worked, and my mom stayed at home with my older brother and me. My older brother and I became close when I was in junior high school and he in high school. My brother, John, is a wonderful person. I could not ask for a better brother. Growing up, he helped me deal with messes I got myself into, and stayed by my side when I explained to my parents what I had done.

My mom learned the silent treatment from her mom. When she got angry at anything, her response was to be silent and not talk to those closest to her; my dad, and my brother, and me. My dad and John handled it better than I by ignoring it or getting away from her. The silent treatment would start because of something I did, or something my father or brother did, or sometimes had nothing to do with any of us. We never knew when or why it would occur or how long it would last.

My dad was busy with his work but when he was home he always showed his love for all of us. He was the principal of the one high school in our town. He started as a music teacher, and then moved onto guidance counselor, assistant principal, and then principal. He loved music, and we always had it on in our house, especially on Sundays.

We lived on the outskirts of a small city on a busy truck route, so there was no real neighborhood. We had a huge back yard where my imagination thrived. My brother and I loved playing outside. Our city consisted of a college and a university. It was a progressive community that sat on one of the Finger Lakes, Cayuga Lake, in upstate New York. There was a lot to do there. I could not have lived in a better community.

I believed from a young age that I was not a good person and longed for others' approval to boost my self-worth. One day, I was excited to have a classmate over to play because it didn't happen often. I thanked my mom. She responded with a gruff, "It isn't that big of a deal, you know." That deflated my excitement. I felt dumb for being excited. Her words had a huge impact on me as a child.

Growing up with a controlling mother created an emotional roller coaster that continued well into adulthood. I took it personally and did somersaults to win back my mother's affection, but to no avail. One minute, I was upbeat because all was well between us, and then the next, I found myself feeling down because she was silent again. I asked what I had done wrong and never received an answer. I thought it bothered my dad sometimes because I saw the hurt and frustration in his expressions. But there was never a discussion, and I usually felt like I walked on eggshells and hoped to stay on her good side.

Children model what they see. So, I don't know if my grandmother's silence upset my mom the way it upset me, but I do know that my mom tried to stay out of her home as often as she could as a child to avoid her mom. I would have done the same thing. However, my mom kept tight reins on me, so leaving the house to play with others was not an option. My only option was to go outside by myself. I felt like I was bad and unlovable. In other words, I believed I was a bad person and didn't deserve what others received. In my mind, I had become this horrible child, and did not know how to change it because I didn't know what was wrong with me in the first place.

My childhood consisted of some fun times, too. For instance, we went to the Appalachian Mountain Club each summer up in Southwest Harbor, Maine. A beautiful, clean lake surrounded the camp, and it offered daily mountain climbs. There were also family events in the evening. We stayed in two tents. My mom and I were in one tent, my dad and my brother were in the other. It was fun! I discovered the joy of picking blueberries there, which I still love doing. I cannot remember a summer vacation where my mom gave the silent treatment to any of us. It was a time when my family bonded. It also faked me out. I would think all was well until we returned home.

Codependency with my mom started at a young age. When I was four, my mom tried to put me in nursery school. No matter how many different ones she tried, I was not content. I often came home crying or refused to stay. Her controlling nature made me so dependent on her that separation was difficult for me. I experienced separation anxiety, which was a result of my codependency, and it cropped up later in my life when I left home for camp and college. I got homesick a lot.

Because of the failed attempts with nursery schools, my mom took me to the ice-skating rink. There, I found my home away from home. My mom started out skating with me but eventually sat in the stands while I skated and took lessons. Skating was right for me, and I am forever grateful that my mom thought outside the box.

I joined the Figure Skating Club in my hometown. I learned what figure skating was all about and fell further in love with the sport. Skating became my source of security. I worked on improving my skills in figure eights, freestyle, and dance. There was nothing more serene in my life than gliding over the ice to music, creating graceful programs, or performing the dances put out by the Figure Skating Association. The association was a figure skating club for serious figure skaters. It allowed skaters more room to skate versus the crowded public skating sessions. There were different tests that we practiced, which helped us qualify for different competitions as we progressed.

The rink was a place where I watched my figure skating abilities improve, and it was something that could not be taken away from me, or so I thought. I even loved the skates themselves with their clean white boots and the beautiful blades that sparkled and glistened as I crossed the ice. It was my healthy addiction!

The rink became my haven. I was content, smiled often, and, developed a talent that made me proud and feel special. It taught me the benefits of hard work, and I challenged myself. If my mom was not talking to me, I forgot about it while I was at the rink and thought about positive things. I don't remember not skating because mom was not speaking to me. She might not be speaking to me in the ride over, but she still took me. Somehow, I always got there.

COMING CLEAN

Figure skating saved my life from age four until I was eighteen. I went to summer skating camps at different college campuses because our rink closed during the summer. While I was not far from home, I did battle with homesickness. I did not know what to do with myself because my mom wasn't there to tell me what to do. Once I worked through the homesickness, I enjoyed myself. One time, my homesickness was so bad my mom brought me home and then without warning, told me I was returning in the next couple of days. I was angry at her and did not know why she was doing that to me. I ended up doing better the second time around. I guess she used "tough love" on me. I had a sweet roommate who was fun on and off the ice. We became inseparable and laughed a lot, which felt wonderful! I made wonderful friends at all the different summer skating sessions I attended. We all shared a love of skating and enjoyed the time spent in the rink working hard at our craft.

I took ballet lessons for a little while to help me develop grace and practice arm and leg extension in all my moves. This helped me a lot. I learned how important simple things like pointing your toe down instead of up made a better impression in a skater's style. The position of my hands and how to move my arms in a flowing manner were all important lessons to help me create my unique, expressive style.

Figure skating gave me a sense of pride. Connecting with music, which I got from my dad, I found I could link it with movement on the ice quite easily. I expressed myself through my skating. I released all my pent up hurt and anger by flowing on the ice and moving my entire body with grace. Jumps and spins were cathartic as well. The negative emotions disappeared, and I had a sense of calm. I found music made me sad, happy, or passionate. On the ice, it encompassed my body majestically.

My dad built a rink in our front yard when my brother and I were young. He froze water on a huge sheet of plastic secured by two by fours. We had a blast. My brother loved hockey, so we shared the space. It was fun to have a rink right out my front door.

One thing that cropped up in my life was that I did not always know where I "fit in." I knew my place ws at the rink. Outside of the rink, my self-esteem was quite low, but I loved helping others. I was a good listener, and the friends I made felt comfortable talking to me. I sympathized with others because I knew what they were feeling.

My empathy for others started at a young age. I will never forget the first parent-teacher conference that my kindergarten teacher requested. There was this sweet little boy who got sent often to the corner for bad behavior. I felt so bad for him! I brought him toys while he was in the corner, and the teacher could not stop me! So, the teacher told my parents, and they explained to me that I had to stop. I was sad but still watched out for him!! He looked so down, and at times had no socks on in the winter. I worried about him! It was a continuous battle between my teacher and me!

Figure skating limited my social life as I got older, but I was willing to sacrifice that. A figure skater's friendships outside of the rink are cut back. I was not allowed to have overnights with friends or go to parties because I had to get up early the next morning for practice. If the rink had closed for the season, I was sometimes allowed to go to a friend's house or have someone over when I was in elementary school. It didn't happen often. My mom scrutinized and found fault in all my friends. This scrutiny continued through my junior and high school years.

My lack of self-worth spilled over into my friendships in grades two through six. My first close friendship as a child was a self-fulfilling prophecy. It is no wonder that I was friends with Kay. She was popular and always surrounded by a group of girls. I wanted to be popular too, so I befriended her. Ironically, as we became closer, Kay got mad at me and gave me the silent treatment like my mom! Once again, I did not know what I had done wrong. Occasionally, I did know why she was mad, like when I did not let her cheat off me during tests, and then I got a better grade than she did. I responded to her the same way I did to my mom. I tried to please her, no matter the cost. I purposely failed tests to be sure she did better than I did.

Once, in the second grade, my teacher, whom I loved at the time, was angry with the class. We were about to take a test, and Kay sat behind me. She tapped me on the shoulder and asked me for a pencil. I turned around to give her a pencil, and the next thing I knew, I was ordered to sit facing the bathroom. I was embarrassed and angry! All I tried to do was silently give Kay a pencil! That day I lost respect for my teacher, and I no longer trusted her. I was humiliated and unjustly punished. Once again, I internalized that I was a bad person and unlikable. I did not understand that people could still like/love someone when they were angry with them. No one said to me, "I am angry with your behavior." I thought if you were mad at me, I must be a bad person.

There were days that Kay came to school, and for no reason, she gave me the silent treatment. What was wrong with me? Again, I walked on eggshells. The worst part was when Kay convinced our mutual friends not to speak to me. I hated going to school when this happened. One day I hid in my closet because I knew no one would speak to me when I got there. It was horrible. I had no one when they ignored me. I was shy and hesitant to find someone else to befriend. I tried, but didn't make any new friends. *Why would I attempt to make other friends when it was clear to me that there was something wrong with me?* I relentlessly tried to get Kay to speak to me again.

My so-called friendship with Kay continued through sixth grade. The fall before I started junior high school (seventh grade), we moved to a brand-new house my parents built. It was an exciting time. I moved about twenty miles away from where Kay lived, so getting together was not easy. My mom had caught onto what Kay was all about and encouraged me to ignore her. I was afraid that if I told her what Kay was doing, she would call Kay's mom. Thankfully, she never did because I would have been fearful of retribution from Kay the following day. It confused me that my mom didn't like it when Kay didn't speak to me, yet she did the same thing.

JUNIOR HIGH SCHOOL

We moved into a great neighborhood during the summer between my elementary years and junior high. It was a nice little neighborhood, and there was hardly any traffic through the area because it was a small development off the main road. Everything was new, and we had more room. There were lots of kids my age in the neighborhood, which was a new experience for me. When we first moved in, there was a party for my mother and me to get to know the neighbors. It was awesome, and I made new friends quickly. Kay and I were in the same assigned school zone; however, I hoped I was free of her. My parents requested that I not be placed in any classes with Kay in junior high, but somehow, I ended up having social studies with her. I tried to avoid her. I didn't want to be removed from the class because I thought Kay would find out and that would be the end of me. Talk about people-pleasing thinking! Two people controlled my life, and I was so afraid to stand up for myself.

I knew my social studies teacher observed the relationship and saw what Kay did. At first, we sat together, but the teacher eventually seated us alphabetically which separated us, much to my relief! I didn't end up switching classes, and with the help of my teacher, learned to detach from Kay. I will never forget this teacher for helping me to step away from a bad friendship.

Junior high school was a new beginning for me. Out of the blue one day, a girl I had met on the bus asked me if I wanted to hang out with her and her friends. I thought it was odd, but I welcomed the invitation. I thought that my parents spoke with my guidance counselor, who set this girl up to seek me out. But that could be my warped thinking: *of course, I was not worthy of having that happen to me. Why would someone want to be a friend of mine?* As that friendship dwindled, I made other friends and came out of my shell. I experienced my first healthy friendship with a girl named Kara. We are still friends to this day.

Growing up is difficult, no matter the circumstances. Where there is a lack of communication and permission to express feelings, the only thing left is to suppress all those thoughts and feelings inside where they can fester and work against a person.

In junior high school, I had two boyfriends. Mike was the one I openly dated. My parents knew about him, but not the other. I first spotted Mike at the rink finishing practice with his hockey team. I looked through our school yearbook to figure out who he was. He attended my school and was a year behind me. We got to know each other, and I fell hard! On our first date, we went to the university to listen to new age music. It was cool, and we enjoyed ourselves. It was awkward because his parents drove us, but it was worth it. It wasn't long after we were dating that he moved, and I was heartbroken. He visited once after that, and I thought we could write back and forth, but that didn't pan out. Recently, we found each other on social media and are friends. Small world.

My addictive behaviors up until junior high school were healthy ones like figure skating. However, in seventh grade, at the rink no less, I learned how to smoke cigarettes. Smoking was my first unhealthy addiction. Unfortunately, I enjoyed it, and my father smoked at home also. I felt cool and accepted by some of the older figure skaters. There was that adolescent need for acceptance. But I grew to enjoy smoking. My mom found a note I wrote to a fellow skater about smoking. She threatened that I would not skate anymore if I didn't stop. I tried to quit, but I didn't want to. I got better at hiding it, and I didn't smoke that often because I couldn't openly buy cigarettes.

MY DAD

My dad was my hero. He worked as a school administrator, and in the summer taught at one of the colleges in our town. When he was around, I felt secure and happy, but he wasn't home much. On the weekends, he would do work around the house, and I loved going on errands with him. He was consistent with me and rarely raised his voice. He was the opposite of my mom. One day mom kicked my brother and me out of the house. When dad came home, he went inside and next thing I knew we could go inside. I don't know what he said to mom, but we were relieved to be allowed back inside.

Dad had been a Navy captain before he met my mom. He was stationed on a minesweeper in WWII and loved the water. The love of water continued with our family. My brother and my dad put together a sailfish, (a small sailboat that you sit on top of with one sail) when I was young. We all loved the water, whether it was the lake or the ocean. Like the rink, the lake was a special place for me. On hot summer days, mom packed up a picnic dinner, and we all went to the lake until dusk, when it would be cooler in the house. We played on the jungle gym and swam to our heart's content. The water made my mom happy, too, which made me feel good. As we got older, our vacations continued to center around water. My love of the ocean and lakes gives me serenity and joy to this day. I am grateful to my dad for that gift!

I loved my dad! I find it interesting that I never said anything to him when mom gave me the silent treatment. In a way, I thought I deserved it. We never discussed my mom's behavior until I was a sober adult. He was unaware of how mom's silent treatment affected me. He was busy working to give us the life we had.

My dad was an excellent educator. In his role as principal, he met with every clique of students in the school so that he knew what their feelings were on different topics. He was proactive versus reactive.

I admire my dad and how he supported kids and staff at the high school I attended. He knew everything that happened in high school within the student body and staff. I listened to my dad relay incidents about his day to my mom at dinner, and I admired how hard he worked to help people. Later, when I entered the field of education, I tried to emulate my dad, by focusing on the needs of my students and by thinking outside of the box.

HIGH SCHOOL

School was not easy for me, but thanks to figure skating, I learned how to be disciplined and did my homework before going to the rink for practice or doing anything else. I tried my best with my school work, but I was not a "book" person. My mom once told my junior high English teacher that," I could confine my daughter to a room with only books in it, and she would engage in something else!" She was right.

In junior high through high school, my parents arranged for me to go into school late so that I could skate before the University's hockey team practiced. I got up very early in the morning, and mom would drive me to the rink, often in her pajamas. It was a fantastic way to start my day. I had the ice almost all to myself. I brought my school clothes, changed, and my mom picked me up and took me to school.

In tenth grade, I attended the high school where my dad was the principal. I continued going to classes late from the rink and enjoyed the social aspects of high school. Having your father as the principal of your high school certainly puts stress on the dating scene! Most boys were afraid to ask out the principal's daughter. I have to admit, I looked so innocent as an adolescent. I walked the halls when, on occasion, I skipped a class holding a piece of paper in my hand that served as a fake pass. No teacher ever questioned me. It was rather fun.

In my junior year, I became friends with a wonderful African-American guy named Bob. I was brought up to accept others regardless of their skin color. We lived in a town with two colleges, and it was a diverse community. Bob and I got to know one another because our lockers were right next to each other. We got along famously. Bob respected my feelings and showed me he cared. I grew to trust him completely. He listened to me, encouraged me, and helped me feel like I was lovable and a good person.

It was the 1970s, so interracial relationships were starting to become more accepted. However, there were a few white kids, and some of my African American female classmates, who weren't exactly pleased. One day, at the start of our friendship, Bob drove me home after school. When we arrived in our driveway, I kissed Bob. He almost had a heart attack! He was worried we would get in trouble if my mom saw us. I thought it was fine and would be fine with both of my parent. I was starting to really like Bob.

When Bob asked me on a date, I knew I had to discuss it with my parents. I was more concerned with my mom's reaction than my dad's. I explained that we were just friends and they were fine with it. Soon after we started going out, we became boyfriend and girlfriend. It surprised me that some teachers raised their eyebrows when they saw us hold hands in the hallways. Other teachers were fantastic. My dad handpicked my teachers and kept me away from those who might be critical of my relationship with Bob and from the few who were critical of his educational philosophy.

Bob was wonderful, and I couldn't have asked for a more special person to be my first true love. We became serious, and my parents worried about that. My mom made comments about my relationship with Bob but never discussed her specific concerns. Once, my mom blew up and demanded, "Don't you listen to any "white" music?!" In response, Kara made an album cover that was white and had a black guy and white girl on it. It said something like, "White Music" as a joke! I needed that comic relief! Bob and I dated throughout high school and went to senior prom together. My parents tried hard to be supportive of us. My mom liked Bob and knew he treated me well. There were probably comments made at different functions my parents attended that pressured them into being concerned. At that time in our history, interracial marriages were not as accepted as they are today. My mom, many years later, said both she and my dad were worried about how the world would treat us and what our children would face if we ever were to marry.

In high school, I could not attend many parties but managed to go to some with Bob, where I witnessed drinking. Neither Bob, nor anyone else pressured me to drink. I would only have one or two. Because of my early morning practices, late nights out on weekends were few and far between. My mom needed to know everywhere I went and what we did, so that put a limit on parties. I sometimes twisted the truth about what we were doing! At the few parties I attended, I didn't feel the need to get drunk at that point in my life. I have heard many alcoholics say that their first drink began their love affair with alcohol. This was not the case with me. I was not exposed to it that much, and was a serious figure skater. However, in June of my senior year, there was a senior camp out. Kara and I got drunk. Bob made sure both Kara and I were safe. The next day was our senior trip, and we were lethargic. It was a lot of fun, but the hangover, not so much!

DIETING AND WEIGHT OBSESSION

During my sophomore-junior years in high school, I gained about ten pounds. I wanted to be thin. As a figure skater, it was important to be on the thin side. Kara and I dieted seriously, but not in a healthy way. We starved ourselves and had rituals we followed, like freezing yogurt, so we ate it slower, only having fruit for lunch, etc. We have a picture of us where our heads looked bigger than our bodies. Losing weight became addictive as it made me more comfortable in my skin. Society put women like Twiggy in front of us. It made teenage girls feel like they had to be thin to be accepted. This influenced me. It was another warning sign of my addictive personality. I remained thin throughout the rest of my high school career. After high school I had periods of time when I struggled again with my weight. Starving myself became difficult to do, but being thin was important to me. It was all about what I showed on the outside that affected my feelings on the inside. It was also about control.... If I could control what went into my body, then I had some means of control over of what felt like an out of control life.

THE MOVE

During my senior year in high school, my dad decided to take a school superintendent job in a nearby town. I was excited for my dad, supported the move, and agreed to attend a new high school. I did not want to stand in his way. I began my second semester at the new high school, which was twenty to thirty minutes away from my hometown. I went from a college town atmosphere to a small farming community! The downtown was so much smaller than what I was used to. It was an abrupt change! The kids were nice and tried to help me adjust. They invited me to their weekend gatherings. I tried to settle in but I missed Bob, Kara, and my other friends tremendously. I had a difficult time adjusting to my classes because they were so different. It felt like there was nothing to do in this town compared to my home town, and it was much harder to get to the rink. After two weeks, I stopped doing homework. I hated the new school and wanted to return to my old high school. Kara and her parents invited me to stay with them. I was excited and prayed my parents would let me. My mom was hesitant but allowed it with the condition I live at home on the weekends. I liked that my Mom would not have control over me at Kara's house, but it made me angry that

I had to agree to go back home every weekend. But I agreed to this in order to my old school. "Although I was delighted that I would graduate from my high school; I was disappointed that my dad would not give me my diploma. He would have if he were still the principal.

Bob and I applied to colleges our senior year. I did not want to attend college because I planned to continue my skating training, and then be a coach. But my parents insisted I attend a two-year junior college, which turned out to be a wise decision on their part. We traveled seven hours to the Boston area and visited two schools. One was too snobby, and the second school felt comfortable and liked the feel of the atmosphere. It was the only college I applied to and thankfully, I was accepted! Bob looked at schools in New York. I think at this point my parents wanted a lot of distance between us, hoping it would eventually end our relationship.

POST-HIGH SCHOOL

The summer of my senior year in high school, Kara and I went to Lake Placid, NY. I went to get more training with excellent skating coaches. We lived in a rooming house and worked as chambermaids at a local hotel. We were there all of two weeks when my back gave me major problems. The chambermaid job put too much stress on my lower back. I later found out it was a major problem.

Consequently, I couldn't skate. I made the trip home lying down in the backseat of the car. Kara had to return home as well, and I felt bad about. I was laid up in bed all summer to keep the pressure off my lower back per doctor's orders. What a hell of a summer that was. I was angry and lost. Underneath the anger was fear. I hoped that the bedrest would do the trick, and I could continue skating in the fall when I went off to college.

Once at college, I was homesick again. I called home and asked if I could visit. My mom responded coldly. We agreed that I would not come home until Thanksgiving. I was upset, and my mom was not empathetic. Maybe that was her attempt at tough love again.

The back pain got worse during the first semester. I hitched a ride with a fellow student at the college and visited Bob at his university. It didn't go very well. I was depressed and not myself. I cried, but could not explain what was going on with me. Bob got frustrated and told me to leave. He dumped me off at my brother's fraternity, where his fraternity brothers took me under their wing. I spent the night and partied hardy with them. The next day, I took a bus to meet with my ride back to my college that never showed. I called my brother in a panic, unsure of what to do. He calmed me down, and I nervously took another bus to Boston. It was late Sunday night when I arrived, and I called a friend from my dorm who picked me up. My relationship with Bob took a downward spiral, and I wouldn't be making any trips again that year.

In late January, I had to come home and faced my first back surgery, a laminectomy. A laminectomy is when the vertebrae in the lower lumbar area are fused to stabilize and stop deterioration. They discovered I had not fused at birth along my pelvis, like everyone else. This caused me to have trouble with balance. I also had an extra bone that was irritating nerves, which caused horrendous pain down my right leg around my pelvis and hip area. The extra bone was used to fuse me properly across my pelvis. It was a grueling recovery. My doctor had an awful, bedside manner that made me mad enough to do what I had to do to recover. Smart move on his part! I had to learn how to walk again because of the deep cut in my muscles.

I had a wonderful professor at college who let me continue my required freshman tutorial via mail. I chose the topic of "Self-Actualization." I had to send him weekly papers and choose a book to read that had special meaning to me. I chose *Jonathan Seagull* because it focused on learning about your true self. I had learned about the self-fulfilling prophecy in one of my high school classes, and it meant a lot to me. The course and book helped me work through a lot of issues. I felt like adults spoke out of both sides of their mouths sometimes. The professor wrote feedback on my papers that was therapeutic for me.

The words poured out of me. I also took a correspondence course in English that helped me earn more credits and pass the time. I loved reading books and discovering the deeper meaning within them.

Once, Bob ran into my mom when he visited me in the hospital. I found out later that she asked Bob not to visit me anymore. I was angry with her. She had no right to do that, but her need to control me, and my life came out, and she dictated what she thought was best for me. Later that summer, when I had recovered enough, I snuck out to see Bob. Bob traveled to my town, and we met in different places. We didn't stay long because I was scared my mom would find out.

Once I got home from the hospital, I walked daily, and eventually, I could climb stairs. My mom did a lot for me throughout the whole ordeal, and I became dependent on her. I appreciated all she did for me. I didn't know what effect my back would have on my skating career, and I had no idea about other careers. I majored in psychology at my junior college, but I didn't know what I could do with that.

I was given many strong pain meds after my surgery. I found taking them helped me to escape. That was another warning sign that I didn't understand. The pain medicine I took made me euphoric and allowed me to sleep. I welcomed anything to avoid thinking about my situation and my future. I learned that a substance helped me deal with my issues. I never discussed my fears about my future with anyone, not even Kara. I never shared the fear and anger I felt with my parents.

Kara came to visit me while I was recovering, and I had her look at a spot on my back that was swollen and blistering hot to the touch. Thankfully, she threatened to tell my parents if I didn't. I told my parents, which lead to a quick visit to the emergency room. I then had emergency surgery to remove a chip of bone that was left by mistake during my initial surgery and had formed a pocket of infection. If my friend had not pressured me to tell my parents and the bubble had burst, it would have ruined the fusion across my pelvis. I will always be thankful to Kara for saving me!

I worked hard at my rehabilitation. I missed an entire skating season that winter. I asked my neurosurgeon about getting back to figure skating. His answer was not what I wanted to hear. I could not do any jumping which felt like a death sentence. I was upset, but again, did not voice it to anyone. I decided to figure it out, but this was the realization of my worst fear. *What was I going to do?* I had more to do if I was going to be a coach. I was scared, lonely, and angry. I stuffed all those feelings. I tried to bargain with the different types of figure skating and thought that I could focus on ice dance in place of the jumps.

One night, while I was bedridden at home, eating my dinner in my room, my parents brought up a small TV. They turned on a figure skating championship. I watched it, and suddenly I became so sad and angry that I threw my plate of food across the room. This was completely out of character for me, and it shocked my parents. I didn't watch any more championships that season! We didn't talk about how I was feeling. I believed it was something I had to face alone. I did not know what I was supposed to do with my life, or with the feelings bottled up inside.

That summer, I convinced my doctor to let me try to get on the ice. I promised not to jump. My hometown rink finally opened in the summer and I went with the focus on ice dance. Well! The arching I needed to use for ice dance hurt and put too much pressure on my lower back. The pain was instant, which told me the ice dancing was not going to be an option. That put the final nail in the coffin for my figure skating career. *Skating was my life and my identity! How could it be just taken away?* The anger and sadness overwhelmed me.

Subsequently, I said goodbye to figure skating and went back to college the following fall. I didn't discuss it with my parents. At school, I talked a little with my roommate, Linda. Mostly, I continued to stuff my feelings. That was when things changed. I had my first dealings with alcohol and pot, my new "friends" that made everything feel okay. When I drank, I fit in. I wasn't angry, and I had fun. I didn't drink socially, though. Little did I know that my drinking pattern was not normal. This period marked the beginning of my drinking career. I learned during my surgery, what pain meds could do, and alcohol was even better because it was accessible.

During the winter of my sophomore year in college, I had an internship in my hometown for a month. I saw Bob quite a bit, but our relationship went downhill fast, and we broke up for good. I became depressed, and my parents had me see a psychologist friend of theirs. I talked about our relationship and my sadness over its end. It was hard getting over Bob. I also discussed my mom's control issues and her overprotectiveness. My parents met with him, and when they returned, my mom was angry with me. Neither of them ever discussed the content of the meeting.

That September, when I returned to college, I was legally able to drink in the state of Massachusetts. My roommate, Linda, and I went to bars in Boston, and there were parties or "mixers" at our school. My college was primarily a girls' school but it had turned coed the year I began, so we were short on the opposite sex! I do not remember ever drinking socially at that time. In other words, I didn't know when to stop. I stopped when I passed out or threw up! In my mind, I was having fun. I did well in school and enjoyed my friendship with my roommate and a couple of other friends.

The next decision that year was what to do in May after I completed my second year of junior college. I had to attend summer courses home at the local state college to complete my associate degree. So, because I didn't have to total amount of credits by the end of my sophomore year I was not allowed to participate in graduation.

I decided to pursue my interest in psychology and majored in rehabilitation counseling when I transferred to another college in Massachusetts for my junior and senior years. I had not chosen a career path yet. I visited the school the summer before classes started to find off campus housing because the dorms were full. There I met my future roommate, Tara. She was friendly, sweet, funny, and upbeat. We got along so well. The college helped us find another roommate to fill the bedrooms and make the rent more affordable. It was a three-story house. The ground floor had an apartment for rent, the owners lived on the middle floor, and my roommates and I lived on the third floor. The house and neighborhood were a bit shabby. The house being close to campus was helpful but we felt very uneasy due to our questionable neighbors…as well as our landlord.

Later in the year, the police arrested a neighbor for rape! When our parents dropped us off that September, they wondered if they were doing the right thing. Fortunately, three guys who attended our school rented the apartment on the first floor. We all grew close, and they watched out for us. Thank God. The following year, Tara and I roomed in the dorms together. Tara was a good influence on me. She didn't drink that much during our two years together. I visited her family and went on vacation with them one spring break. Tara had a great family, and I loved being with them, and finally she was a friend that my mom liked!

I had a boyfriend named Jim for part of my sophomore and junior years in college. He partied a lot, and his father was a heavy drinker. Jim and I smoked pot and drank regularly. It was a doomed relationship, and I was under a cloud of substances. *If I was not happy with my life at that point, how could I be happy with this guy?* I became depressed. I broke it off, and the cloud lifted temporarily. It was not his fault at all. We both enjoyed alcohol too much.

For the next two years, I drank almost every weekend. The purpose was to get drunk, and I didn't think there was anything wrong with that. I still hadn't found anything to replace figure skating. When I arrived home after my junior year, my mom bluntly pointed out that I had gained weight. So, I ran to lose weight I had gained from drinking. Running became challenging and also soothing to me. I dated a great guy whom I went to high school with that summer, and we ran together. That summer, I managed my drinking because I LOVED to run and didn't want to be hung-over the next day and not be able to run! I stopped running when my senior year started and my summer relationship ended when we both returned to our colleges.

DEPRESSION

I exhibited signs of depression at an early age. In high school, I tried to slice my wrists once. It did not go very deep, but it was a definite cry for help, although I did not share with anyone other than Bob, and possibly Kara. It was around the time we were about to move. I enjoyed feeling the pain released when I sliced. But it hurt too much as I cut deeper, and I did not want to kill myself. I didn't know what depression was; I knew I was sad. I wondered why I was not happier.

Many alcoholics suffer from depression. I drank to wash away hurtful feelings and events. I was never allowed to express my anger in my home. Only my mom could. Hence, I learned at an early age to stuff everything. Between stuffing my feelings and depression running in my family, I suffered silently, filled with self-doubt. But I didn't know what I didn't know! I looked at others and longed to feel self-confident and happy! I felt like I was on an island. I didn't know that I could talk about my feelings and that there was help. I was ashamed of my feelings. I acted "as if" things were okay. It was exhausting.

Depression is sneaky. I could still have fun at times, but then sink back into the depths of sad feelings. Sometimes I slept to keep the sad thoughts away. But my depression was always in the background, and sometimes in the forefront and so profound. I had no idea that others did not feel this way and that my feelings were not normal and that there was help!

In college, drinking became my coping mechanism. When I drank, everything felt okay. I blacked out in college, but thankfully, I had friends who watched out for me. Once I was sobered up from a night of drinking, my feelings were still there, and I had to deal with them.

I continuously worried that someone was mad at me. If people didn't show me approval of some sort, I panicked and thought I had done something wrong.

I constantly asked those close to me "are you mad at me?" The answer was, usually, "No, why?" Nevertheless, I was paranoid that people didn't like me. I practiced constant people pleasing, trying to gain approval so I would feel okay. I never outwardly disagreed with someone unless the topic was about me. I disagreed in my mind. I didn't share my opinions for fear of making the person mad. However, friends came to me with their problems, and if it was someone else's issue, I could give honest feedback and suggestions. I was able to handle other people's problems but not mine.

Throughout college I felt "different." I was emotionally frozen. I was sadder than I was in high school. My alcohol abuse made things worse. I did make some wonderful friends in college and got back in touch with a few of them once I became sober. They were and are wonderful people, and we had good times. One night, we couldn't sleep, so we took off in my Oldsmobile cutlass convertible and went to a nearby park. There were several signs and sawhorses that we found humorous. We proceeded to put some of them in my car and brought them back to the dorm to decorate a part of our hall and bathroom. Others did not find it as funny as we did.

I was bored one night, and I had my father's cute

little car, a Buick Opel, while my car was getting repaired. The compact size was a blast. I took one of my friends for a little ride on the sidewalks around the campus. I looked in my rearview mirror and saw one of the campus police running on foot after us. I accelerated so he could not catch us. We disappeared for a while that night before we returned to campus. Mid-morning the next day we got a phone call. It was the office of the campus police. They asked if the Opel belonged to me and I confirmed this.

The man asked, "Were you driving last night?"

I responded, "No, but my cousin, who is visiting me had my car."

There was a pause, "Well, we won't issue a ticket this time, but please let your cousin know that this type of reckless driving is not allowed on campus!"

I assured him I would convey his message and hung up. My roommate and I laughed so hard! But I didn't try that again either! That was good clean fun, and no alcohol was involved. Luckily, I was let off the hook by campus security.

Academically, I was more successful in college than in high school. But I couldn't find anything to replace my love and focus of figure skating. There was a hole in my life. I was going through the motions of life and doing what others wanted.

After my freshman year, I loved being away from home. When I returned home for the summers, I rebelled against my mom's control. I had been fending for myself at college, but at home, I was under her control again, which did not sit well with me. I walked on eggshells but was learning to fight back, which never got me anywhere.

My boyfriends throughout college were fun but not like Bob. Marriage was never on my mind. I hadn't met "the one" after Bob at that point. Although I yearned for my mom's approval, she never approved of any of them.

POST-COLLEGE

      I floundered a little the summer after I graduated from college. I skipped from one job to the next. I was dating a guy who was still in college, and I had not moved back home to New York State. I found a job as a nanny in a town near my college in Massachusetts. I worked for a family consisting of two boys and a father. I was a live-in nanny during the week and had weekends off. The dad, John, was an actuary for a major insurance company. It was my job to run the household and care for his six and ten-year-old boys. They had tragically lost their mom in a car accident before their move to Massachusetts from Connecticut. It was a sad situation, and I became fond of the boys.

      The youngest, Nick, didn't talk to me for the first few weeks. Nick's silence had been a game that had started with his mom and her work colleagues. Nick would not speak to them, and they found fun ways to get him to talk. Then, it became a serious problem. Since his mom's death, it had become even more serious. Finally, he trusted me enough to speak to me. Nick started first grade in a new school that fall. The first day of school, Nick came home with wet pants. I asked him about it, and he reluctantly told me that he didn't want to tell anyone he needed to go to the bathroom because he wasn't talking to anyone. This poor little boy! The next day, I called the school and spoke to the guidance counselor. I explained the situation, and we worked out a signal that alerted the teacher that he needed to go to the bathroom. The counselor and I worked together, and Nick adjusted gradually to his new school and surroundings.

Taking care of Nick and Carleton was stressful as they worked through the death of their mom. John was a good person, but worked long hours and often didn't make it home for dinner. I drank one or two and sometimes three gin and tonics around dinner time to relax. I never got totally drunk, but I looked forward to those drinks and that buzz.

At one point, Carleton, the older brother threw a chair at me out of anger after coming home from school one day. Something had happened at school, and he wouldn't talk about it. I kept pushing him, and the chair got thrown. Of course, I took the blame for it, let the boy have his space, and then went back and apologized! He had been teased about his name at school and was hurt and angry. We discussed it and came up with ways to handle it in the future. We both learned from the situation.

As I worked with the guidance counselor at Nick's school, I knew I would love that type of job. I discussed this with my parents and applied to my college for their master's degree program in guidance counseling. I am not surprised that I chose this as a career. I admired my dad and his role as an educator. I liked the thought of working in the field of education, but never wanted to be a teacher. I was accepted and would attend a one-year program in the fall.

My mom called me in the spring before I started my master's degree program and suggested I go to California to stay with my brother and sister-in-law for the summer. I loved this idea, and in May, I left my job to go to San Luis Obispo. I stayed with my brother and sister-in-law initially, found a job, and later moved into an apartment with two other girls.

My drinking continued, but for the most part, was only on the weekends, and I was not blacking out. I had a good summer with my brother and sister in law. I got to know my sister in law's family, whom I grew to love. I enjoyed living in California. I worked at a fast-food place, then in a nursing home. My brother and sister-in-law showed me different sites in California, and I loved getting to know my roommates. I didn't have a car but rode a bike to work each day.

During that summer, I kept a long-distance relationship going with my college boyfriend Paul. My mom called one day and told me Paul was no longer welcome in their home. She felt that he was not good enough for me and didn't treat me well. She had no evidence to substantiate it! I was devastated and angry with my mom for trying to control my relationship. I played her game and refused to speak to her after that. I shared this information with Paul, who broke up with me a few days later. I did not blame him, but I had no part in what happened. It was their battle against each other, and I was the one who became the pawn. I was furious with my mom.

I refused to take phone calls from her for a week, and eventually, she spoke to my brother to convince me to take her call. She said she was sorry, but it was too late. I told her Paul had broken up with me, and I hoped she was happy about that. My summer ended, and I had saved enough money for my flight home. I gained some weight, and when I got off the plane, mom's first comment was, "You've gained weight!" Thank you, mom!

My parents had moved to the town next door to my college, where my dad had taken a new position as superintendent of a school system. So, I was uncertain if I would be commuting to college for my master's degree.

Once back at their house, and before classes started, mom made me go to weight watchers. I was humiliated. I needed to lose about ten pounds again. I was angry and felt horrible about myself. I felt the disapproval of my mom and wished she would have said things like, "I love you; I support you no matter what; I am proud of you. Let me help you lose some weight if you want to."

My parents and I discussed my living closer to campus for my master's degree program. A friend I graduated from college with lived in my college's city and was looking for a roommate. I took her up on it as the rent was affordable. I was grateful to be able to live close to school and be on my own. My parents put my brother and me through undergraduate college, but the deal was that after that, it was on us. I was surprised and thankful that my parents were willing to help me with some of my tuition to get the education I needed to do what I was meant to do.

At the beginning of my master's program I met with my advisor, who was the head of the guidance counselor program.

He stated, "I don't think you are going to make it in this program."

I was stunned. I asked, "Why"?

"I don't think you have what it takes to be successful" Well! This made me furious with him and motivated me to prove him wrong, and I did. After two internships, one at a junior high school, and one at a high school, he had to eat his words. My course work and my internship reviews were excellent.

At the end of our program, he approached me at a gathering and said, "I need to eat my words. You have done an excellent job."

I admired him for admitting he was wrong. He earned my respect that day.

During that year, Bob visited me, and we discussed getting back together. We even discussed marriage. When I got the nerve to tell my parents that Bob and I were back together, long-distance, of course, my mom went ballistic. She accused me of planning the whole thing. She said that I used them to get my master's degree and then planned to marry Bob. She made no sense, but she said some hateful things to me. What hurt the most were her constant assumptions that I was dishonest, and that I had ulterior motives. I didn't, and I had a hard time lying because of the guilt I felt. I slammed out of the house and shut my mother out. I was scared to go against my parents and lose them, so I decided to break it off with Bob, which was hard. It was odd that during many of these instances with my mom, my dad was never a part of the conversation.

My mom and I didn't talk for at least a week and a half and then she called me. I responded to her coldly. She apologized and I said, "It doesn't matter because we broke it off." Per usual, when I tried to please my mom, I was miserable. I was placing my wants and desires secondary to hers.

After this, I again partied hardy on the weekends. And again I drank to get drunk. Several times my heavy drinking led me to go home with someone and sleep with them. I thought that maybe if I slept with a guy, it would lead to a relationship. Wrong! I was gullible and believed their sweet talk! Ugh! Alcohol helped me socialize at big parties where otherwise, I was uncomfortable.

Although I had been promiscuous while I was in school, I naively believed an unwanted pregnancy would never happen to me. I always insisted on a condom, but my naivety was shattered when I discovered I was pregnant. I was beside myself. I never discussed the pregnancy with the father and decided my best option was an abortion.

The procedure was the worst. My blood pressure dropped a lot, and I held in all my feelings. At one point, I burst out in tears.

During the procedure, I heard the nurse say, "Oh, thank God, your blood pressure came back up."

I felt loss, shame, and remorse for doing that and for being so irresponsible in the first place. It made me grow up fast. I felt I would never be forgiven by God for doing this.

Out of anger, I told the father I had the abortion. He was flabbergasted. He was upset I had the abortion without talking to him. I probably should have told him, but I felt the decision was mine to make alone. I didn't want a relationship with a man I spent one night with because I got pregnant. I knew I was not ready to raise a child. I had not shared my feelings or thoughts with anyone other than one friend. To this day, I ask for forgiveness for taking the life of an innocent child. After that, I made sure I was using birth control and didn't just count on a condom alone.

MY FIRST SCHOOL
COUNSELOR POSITION

My first job after receiving my master's degree was as an aide in a high school special needs program. In mid-winter, I interviewed and got my first position as a guidance counselor.

The first day I walked into high school, I heard a man bellow, "Where do you think you are going?"

He was yelling at me!

I responded, "I am the new special needs counselor."

His said, "Oh, my apology, Miss."

He let me know that I looked like one of the kids which I took as a compliment!

My position was at a middle and high school, and I worked only with special needs students. It was in a remote, disadvantaged community in upstate New York. Some of the families that I made home visits to were lacking in basic living necessities. I will never forget visiting a father who worked for the postal service. He and his son lived in a house with dirt floors and no electricity. I was astonished, but also in awe of how these people survived and seemed happy in their simple lives. This was a major education in and of itself. I loved working with my students and their families. It was hectic working between two schools and meeting the demands, but I was young and could handle it.

As scared of life as I was, I kept moving forward. I had a career! But I was scared of life in general, and felt ill-equipped to handle it. When I showed up to my job, I put on the mask of professionalism. I knew what I was doing in my job (although I was not as confident as I looked), but not in my personal life. I was petrified the first time I had to stand up in front of a class. I didn't know this was a job requirement, and it was the reason I didn't become a teacher! Despite authentic fear, I went up there. I didn't realize at the time that I had guts underneath that fear, and that someone was watching over me and guiding me, despite myself.

I rented an apartment in a house in town. I was not too far from my hometown. I got back in touch with Kara, who had gotten married. I loved living close to my hometown. I had adopted a dog, Toby, whom I loved! Toby, however, didn't like riding in the car. Consequently, rides to see my parents, seven hours away, were extremely noisy. Once on the highway, Toby did better with the cars going the same way, but in two-way traffic, forget it! She barked nonstop! I wanted to pull my hair out. Nothing I tried helped. Toby was part Collie and part St. Bernard. She was a love and great company for me as I was quite lonely in this remote town.

I was grateful too for my apartment that was near Lake Ontario. I loved being close to water again. I bought my first brand new car after my first year of work. I was so proud of that car! I bought it with standard drive and forced myself to learn as I left the car lot! It was my pride and joy. I could afford my apartment, a car payment, and pay small amounts on the loan I had taken out for my master's degree.

I met a teacher named Sharon, who became a wonderful friend. She was a special education teacher at the high school, and she and I developed a work/study program for the high school's mentally challenged students. It worked well for the kids. I made other friends as well, and we smoked pot and drank on the weekends. It was usually one day on the weekend. I used pot more than I drank at this point in my life.

It was my second year at this job when the school district hired a drug and alcohol counselor for the high school. At the time, I was dating a guy named Ed, who was kind and fun. He worked for an airline, and I had been introduced to him by a friend at work. But when Don, the drug and alcohol counselor, came along, my focus did a one-eighty. Don and I became interested in each other and began dating. I broke up with Ed, who wanted to marry me. Looking back, I would have been so much better off with Ed, but Don was exciting to me. Smoking pot and having alcoholic drinks became a regular past time, even on the weeknights. Don and I saw each other daily, and eventually, I moved in with him. The beautiful house he rented was on a bay of the lake. I loved being there. When I took a swim, Toby swam beside me. I looked forward to coming home to light up a joint or drink. I didn't drink to the point of oblivion as the pot was my focus. Often, I would have a joint in the car that I smoked on the way home.

My parents called me at my apartment, but I was never there. When they finally reached me, they were angry that I was not living there anymore. They were unhappy that Don and I lived together. They visited one weekend and met Don. My mom hardly spoke to me, but I stuck to my guns and tried to ignore her anger. Don was hard for others to understand. He kidded around or gave short answers. He told me he was in remission from cancer, had served in Vietnam, and had been dishonorably discharged. To me, this was exciting. While we were together, I

noticed that throughout our relationship, he never saw a
doctor for his alleged cancer.   In the back of my mind, I
thought he was not completely truthful with me, but I
ignored it. As the drug and alcohol counselor, he
confiscated pot from students and tried to counsel them to
get help if they struggled with drugs or alcohol abuse.
 Later in our relationship, he gave me the confiscated pot.
I am ashamed of this, but the disease of addiction had me.
At the time, I didn't care that it was wrong. My morals
had begun to deteriorate.

Don told me he had graduated from the
University of Alabama and had played football there under
Bear Bryant. He also said that had gotten his master's
degree in social work from the University of Rochester.
Both his parents had died young, and he had an older
brother and sister. His brother had quadriplegia because of
a drunk driving accident. He was divorced and had two
kids. It was a disjointed family.

One day, I received a letter from my mom stating
that she and my dad wanted us to get married or I was not
allowed to visit them again. As I read this letter to Don, he
suggested we get married. I was thrilled and surprised
because Don had said he was not interested in marriage. I
called my parents, and they were pleased with our decision.
However, I was letting my mother call the shots again. My
brother flew out for the small wedding overlooking the
ocean on Cape Cod. I had a simple dress and ring, but
Don did not want to wear a ring. We got married over
school vacation in April, and we drove to Florida for our
honeymoon. I downplayed the whole wedding ceremony
for Don. I thought if I kept it low key, I would not scare
him away. A church wedding was out of the question. I
don't recall Don having any friends, so besides his brother
and sister, I do not know who he would have invited to
our wedding. This also should have felt strange to me, but
it did not. I ignored a lot.

While in Florida, Don had to make a lot of student progress notes that were due because he was being reviewed by the state when we returned to work. I was bored silly and realized he made stuff up in his notes. I had never seen anything like this, but once again, I kept my mouth shut. We left Florida and drove to New Orleans. I had never been there before. There were so many bars and drinking occurred day and night in the streets. That night, I woke up and discovered that he was not in the room. He didn't sleep much. When he returned, I was worried. I asked where he had been. He finally admitted that he had gone to strip joints. Trying to be cool about it was hard. I was hurt and angry. I asked him to stop, and he said he would, but a couple of nights later, he went out again. I was afraid he went back to the strip clubs. I never found out if he went again, and I didn't want to ask.

Our relationship was okay, for the first few years, but it was superficial. Don was antisocial and never had friends outside of work. He didn't want to get together with Kara and her husband, so that relationship ended. I also noticed that he was not doing his job. Others noticed it, too. Don decided to leave his job at the high school. I overheard a conversation between my boss and the school psychologist who said he had been asked by Don to write him a recommendation. The psychologist said he did not feel comfortable doing that. That confirmed my thoughts that Don was not doing his job properly.

I had a job, and Don did not. It put stress on our relationship. My job was hectic, and I became burnt out. Perhaps I was burnt out from carrying the burden of being the sole breadwinner. I drank and smoked quite a bit. There were times when I got high when I traveled from one school to another. I eventually left my job too. I was not happy, but I didn't know what to do about it. I was lost again.

MY NEXT CAREER

Don and I moved near my parents in Massachusetts. They introduced us to their neighbor, who was building an ice cream franchise and was looking for managers. Unenthused at the prospect, but knowing we needed work, we agreed to do it. It was a huge mistake. I hated it, and we barely got by financially. The owner was egotistical and rude to me because I was a woman. I took a course at the University of Massachusetts in my field of counseling to keep current in my career. Towards the end of this job experience, Don told me he had punched the owner in the face. I was not there, and no one ever told me this happened besides Don. I was extremely upset and didn't know if the owner would press charges. He didn't. I thought he would have, and that made me wonder if it really happened. I think it was another lie.

We looked for work in our fields, and I applied for a guidance position in Maine. Don also wanted us to apply to a job as house parents at an all-boys school for the emotionally challenged. I was offered the job in Maine, and we were also offered the house parents job. Don wanted us to take the house parents job because we would both be employed. I was not comfortable taking the job, but I wanted to please him.

The boy's school we lived in was just outside of Boston. It was a three-story home in a nice neighborhood. We had six boys in our house, and their ages ranged from nine to eighteen.

I grew to love the boys and slowly adjusted to the job. They were a challenge in many ways, but they found a place in my heart quickly. The first night, when one of the boys pulled the fire alarm, I realized we were in for quite a ride. I still had Toby, my dog, which the boys all loved. Each night, I sat on the stairs between the boy's rooms and read to them. I found it helped them let go of their inner turmoil and go to sleep. There was one boy, Christian, who was a bear to wake up in the morning. He would swear up a storm, and it took forever. He loved Toby, so I enlisted her help to wake Christian up each morning. I put a biscuit near Christian's head, and Toby jumped up on the bed, ate the treat, and kissed Christian. Toby worked miracles, and we proceeded to have wonderful wakeups. As Christian lay there petting Toby, we would sit and talk while Christian woke up.

During that first year, we were asked by the administration to provide our degree credentials and where we attended college and graduate school as they were doing a salary review. I found it odd that Don put down only his bachelor's degree information. Then he whited it out and listed his master's degree information. About a week later, our boss called us into his office. He sat us down and explained he had called Don's schools and found he had never graduated from either school! He fired us both. I was shocked. I had to be told by someone else that my husband had lied to my family and me about his education. *Why would he do this?* I didn't say anything, but tears rolled down my cheeks. We left the office, and I was speechless. We got in our car and drove, and Don started apologizing. I couldn't believe this was happening. I could not believe he had lied to me about this! My respect for Don was at an all-time low. *What were we going to do from here? Do I tell my family?* I was in a state of shock and plopped one foot in front of the other. I was humiliated and didn't want to show my face on the school campus. I had nothing to do with this whole mess, but I was guilty by association. In the evenings, when all the boys were asleep, I would go out to the porch and sit in silence and smoke a joint. Don and I didn't discuss it. I am not sure why. There was not a lot to say. I continued to stuff my feelings and kept the "secret." It was like tiptoeing around the elephant in the room, which was my life with Don! We remained in the house in our jobs through the end of the school year and through the summer program on campus. We had to find other employment again.

I managed to get a couple of recommendations from friends I had at the school who knew I was not a part of the lie. I applied to jobs in guidance. Don did not look for other jobs. He had learned wood carving from a fellow houseparent and was consumed doing this. I applied to a job on Nantucket and flew over for the interview. I got the job, and at the end of the summer, we moved to Nantucket.

My new position as a guidance counselor was different from my previous job. I was assigned a study hall at the end of the day and had lunch duty. Being a counselor one minute and a disciplinarian another did not sit well with me. I was trained as a counselor, not to discipline students. Some thought that wealthy families made up the island community. Those who remained on the island year-round were mostly lower-income, and some were running from circumstances in their lives. The student body was a tough crew for the most part. During my first week, I was outside convincing a student to give her knife to me. That was my first clue of what might be in store for me.

Meanwhile, I became more depressed. I drank each day after work. Don was not seeking employment. He went down to the docks and carved little ducks and gave them to people. I was angry with him and my situation. He got mad at me because I had long hours at school. I tried to do a good job.

One evening, I called my parents sobbing. I was miserable. They didn't know we lost our previous job. I kept a lot from them. Don was becoming verbally and emotionally abusive. And, I didn't realize I deserved better. My Mom knew I was depressed. Thankfully, she did some research to connect me with a psychiatrist in Hyannis. I called in sick on the day of my appointment and took the ferry to the mainland to meet with him. He immediately put me on medication. It helped a little, but I was already over the edge. My mom came to visit us and stayed for a while. I was so depressed, and I wanted to sleep all the time. I would wake up to go to work but would end up crying and call in sick.

After a week of not being able to work I called my psychiatrist. He suggested I leave my job. My parents said I could return to their house and let Don take care of moving our things. Our marriage was not good. I had never thought of leaving him. But I needed a break. Don remained on the island until he could get someone to help him move our things. It wasn't much, because the rental house came with furniture. I continued to see my helpful psychiatrist. I was extremely depressed. I was not suicidal, but I was in a bottomless pit where I could not see the light. I was "frozen" in my thoughts. I drank almost every evening with my parents, but not to the point of oblivion. It certainly took the edge off for the evening.

The holidays were fast approaching, and Don said he was trying to find employment in Hyannis. We had no money, but Don told me he was carving some gifts for my parents for Christmas. I didn't trust him as he had not been following through with much these days, including employment. A couple of days before Christmas, Don arrived at my parents'. He was pleased with himself and opened the trunk of his car to show me a couple of mirrors that had shells carved on top of the frame. I did not believe he had made them himself and challenged him, which made him very angry. I didn't have any other gifts to give my parents, so we gave them the mirrors. My parents graciously accepted them, but I still thought Don had bought them. Things were tense between us. My brother and his family were visiting us from California. I had such a hard time holding my emotions in check. I was in tears all the time. After Christmas, my parents asked Don to leave. It was too stressful, and I was relieved they did that. When he asked if that was what I wanted, I nodded my head and said yes. He stormed out. Don had done a number on me, always turning things around so that it was my fault. I was intimidated by his anger. And, after being hit once early on in our marriage, I never trusted it wouldn't happen again, although I had told him, "you will never do that again!"

In the meantime, my parents were building a house in Chatham, Massachusetts, right next to Hyannis. I gradually began to feel better and wanted to return to my life with Don and give it another try. My parents kindly offered to let us live in their house even before they had a chance to live there. Don still had no job, but eventually worked the overnight shift at a grocery store stocking shelves. My parents gave us a move out deadline. As that deadline approached, we did not have enough money for first and last month's rent. Against my better judgment, I cashed in my life insurance policy, given to me by my parents when I graduated from college. I also closed out my retirement account from New York State. We found a cute little house in Barnstable to rent. It was then that I started looking for a job. I did not feel well enough to go back to guidance counseling, so I found a job as a receptionist at a nearby veterinarian's office. They treated and boarded animals. I liked that job and loved my coworkers. It was the perfect job for me at the time.

I discussed my relationship with Don with my

psychiatrist. There was tension between us, and I didn't believe anything he said. We needed marriage counseling, but my psychiatrist recommended that Don should go to individual counseling first. Don agreed, or so I thought. He told me he had started counseling.

Don told me his counselor said I needed to back off. I reported this to my psychiatrist, who asked who Don was seeing and I told him. The next week, when I saw my doctor, he told me Don was not seeing a therapist. Don had mistakenly told me he was using my mental health office. My doctor had checked with all the therapists, and no one knew of Don. Once again, Don had lied to me in a major way. I had naively trusted him one more time. I was furious and sick to my stomach. *Who was this person I had married?*

It took me a couple of days, but I decided to get a divorce. When Don came home the next day, I told him I was leaving and wanted a divorce. I told him I knew he was not seeing any therapist, and that was the final straw. He did not deny that he was not seeing anyone. There was no reaction from him at all. I went to see my parents and brought Toby to their house. I told them all the lies Don had told me, and that I was going to divorce him. They were astounded at the lies and relieved I was divorcing him. I was ashamed, angry, sad, and afraid. I was the first and only one in my family to get a divorce. My father helped me find a lawyer, and I filed. I continued to work at the animal hospital. I moved the furniture I wanted, that was given to me by my parents, out of the house while Don was at work. It was a difficult time, but I was relieved the chaos was gone.

After staying with my parents for about four months, I knew I could not afford to live on my own, given my income. I needed to go back into guidance counseling. I applied to a temporary, one-year guidance position in New Hampshire. The person I would be replacing took a year off to try real estate. While I knew I might be looking for a job again in a year, I thought it might be the best way to re-enter the field which I had been away from for three years.

I applied to other jobs but was given the job opportunity in New Hampshire. Dad drove up with me to help me find an apartment that allowed dogs. At the veterinarian's office, one of the technicians had found a stray, pregnant, long hair calico cat that I fell for at first sight. I adopted her, and "Calli" had her babies at the animal hospital. After that, they spayed her for me. The technicians and one of the veterinarians put my maiden name on the cage so that the owner didn't know they were doing this out of the goodness of their hearts! Before I left the animal hospital, the owner told the other employees to take his credit card and take me for a goodbye meal. Then, we went back to one of my co-worker's homes, and they all gave me gifts. They were an unbelievable group of people whom I will never forget. It was a great experience for me and what I needed at that time in my life.

Once I moved into my apartment in southern New Hampshire, Toby and Calli learned to adjust to each other. The two of them became best buds, and they were my support system.

Up until this point, my drinking was manageable, although I still drank to get drunk. While working at an animal hospital on Cape Cod, there was usually one night each weekend that I would get drunk with my friends. Moving to a new place, with new people and new expectations was nerve-racking for me. I usually went back to the Cape on weekends with animals in tow to see my parents.

INCREASE OF MY DISEASE

In my new life, I was scared and lonely. I hoped I could perform well at my job and threw myself into it. I found that wine in the evenings helped. It masked my feelings of loneliness and fear for the night so that I could sleep. It was the first time I drank by myself. The court date for my divorce was on my birthday. I asked my lawyer to change it. In no way did I want to be reminded of my divorce each year on my birthday. I took back my maiden name, and I thought that Don didn't know where I moved. On my birthday in September, a bouquet arrived at work. I opened the card, and my hands started to shake. The flowers were from Don. I threw them in the trash, much to the surprise of my coworkers. I was scared. *How did he find out where I lived?* I figured he called the animal hospital and they innocently gave out the information. He called me at my apartment to let me know that he had bought a yellow jeep. He knew I had wanted a jeep and he wanted to show it to me. I said no and to leave me alone. For the next few weeks, I looked over my shoulder and wondered if I would see him or a yellow jeep, but thankfully, it never happened.

The day of my divorce came. The court hearing was on the Cape, and the day before I went to my parents' house. I was a nervous mess. I did not want to see Don again. I got a phone call from one of the school counselors I worked with, and I wept over the phone. She calmed me and told me to go in with my head up high. I am grateful for her advice and support. My father accompanied me to court. As I entered the building, I saw my lawyer and my soon to be ex-husband, talking and smiling. This did not sit well with me. My lawyer saw me and walked away from Don. Don and I had to go before the judge by ourselves, and my lawyer would be in the background if needed. I was even more nervous.

The judge asked, "What are your reasons for a divorce?"

Don said nothing; he stood there and smiled.

I spoke up, "Irreconcilable differences, sir."

The judge asked, "Is there any way you can work your differences out?"

I replied adamantly, "No, sir."

That was that!! We both left the courtroom; I spoke briefly with my lawyer and then walked out of the building. Don said a cordial goodbye to both my dad and me. I wanted to smack him. We went back to my parent's house, and I had several drinks and cried. I was ashamed for divorcing someone I had once loved, and angry because I was in this position with no other alternative. I returned to work and struggled for a week or two. I was lonely and ashamed that I had married Don and then couldn't make it work. I felt like a failure and an idiot. I occasionally saw my psychiatrist on Saturdays when I visited my parents. Then it got too hard, so I started looking for therapists close to where I lived.

My drinking became more frequent. Wine at night ended up being a regular occurrence. I became good friends with Sandy, the secretary in the guidance office. I liked my job, but felt I was not good enough to be a school counselor. I doubted myself and still didn't know where I belonged. In the back of my mind, I wanted to skate. That loss was ever-present.

My friendship with Sandy was great. I was always at her house, and I enjoyed her kids and husband. We enjoyed our drinks but had a lot of fun that didn't involve alcohol. Our friendship continued until she and her family moved to Massachusetts. My job was going well. However, I felt that if people got to know me, they would realize I was lousy at my job and a bad person. There was one man I dated for a little while. There were no real sparks, but I was thrilled someone wanted to date me, a divorced woman. I felt like I was damaged goods. This man's interest in me was the ego boost I needed. As the relationship progressed, he became forceful with me sexually, and that did it. I ended it immediately. I was not going to be vulnerable to any man again. He was confused because I didn't tell him why I was ending it. He was a colleague of mine at the school, and one day after I had broken it off, I came into work and found a toothbrush in my mailbox. I had used it once when I stayed overnight at his house. He was angry and wanted to embarrass me, and it worked.

A colleague referred me to a therapist who was the worst therapist I had ever seen. He ridiculed me for my thoughts or actions. The friend who referred me ended up suing him. I quit seeing him and fell further into my hole. I did not seek therapy for a while after that experience.

I had many emotions stuffed inside. I tried to survive as an adult, but I carried a lot of shame, self-doubt, sadness, loneliness, and anger. The anger rarely came to the surface. I drank my problems and feelings away. At first I didn't miss much work even though I drank in the evenings. I did catch many illnesses that were going around the school. I tried hard to be good at my work and would go in even when I was sick. As my drinking continued though, I did miss days due to hangovers.

In the spring of my first year, the person whose job I was filling came in to meet with the principal. I was nervous and wondered if I would be searching for another job. But luckily, I learned I could stay in my position permanently. I was relieved when the principal informed me that my predecessor was resigning and the job was mine.

After my fourth year, I obtained tenure, like I did with my first job in upstate NY. I decided to purchase a home instead of spending my money on rent.

MOVING ON

My parents were instrumental in helping me find
and put a down payment on a condo in a town nearby. I
was relieved to not live in the town I worked in anymore,
where I felt everybody watched what I bought and how I
dressed on the weekends! I also did not like having to run
into my students' parents, who thought they could take
fifteen minutes to talk about their child's problems.

I loved my new condo and was happy to be
established. I did feel a lot of guilt that my parents had to
help me with a down payment. I am grateful to both my
parents for all they did for me. They never complained
about helping me get on my feet. They never complained
about all they did to help me. I tried to make sure they
knew how much I appreciated it.

Toby, Calli and I settled into our new home. I
walked Toby each day, and Calli loved sitting out on the
deck. Toby had a difficult time with fireworks and thunder
as she aged. She and I were up several nights surviving the
noise. I loved Toby, but Don had done a number on her
when I was away from the house. I found out from my
friend Sharon who had visited me, when we were on the
Cape, from upstate New York. She was at my house when

I was at work, and she saw how abusive Don was to Toby. He would yell at her, which would scare her. I noticed how scared of him she was once I got home. This happened near the end of our marriage when he was angry at me, so he took it out on poor Toby.

There were two people who worked in the sales office below my condo. One day, I watched the male salesperson leaving in his suit and dress coat. I wondered, *is he married and going home to his wife?* He walked with such confidence and looked relaxed. I wondered how that felt. The woman who sold the condo to me was a sweetheart. Her daughters attended the school where I worked. Small world!

A couple of months after I moved into my condo, I received a call from the male salesperson in office of the condominiums where I lived. His name was Dan, and he asked me out. I was shocked! The guy who I thought was nice looking and looked stable was asking me out? I accepted. On my first date with Dan, I was a bit nervous, so I had drinks while we were out, but they were mostly beers. We danced a little and enjoyed each other. I learned he had been in the Air Force, and when he returned, he got his real estate license. We continued to date, and I loved his sense of humor. He was so kind to me. We did fun things and enjoyed each other. He was even-keeled, with a solid character. I needed that type of person in my life. I fell fast for Dan.

If we went for a cookout with Dan's family, I needed a drink or two beforehand. He didn't know that I had those drinks. I was insecure and wanted to socialize. Large groups overwhelmed me because conversations drain people who have depression and anxiety. I needed alcohol to help me act "normal!" I was on antidepressants, but they did not work when I drank! I didn't know you could tell your doctor that antidepressants were not working; I thought they were always working at their maximum potency.

My parents met Dan at the Boston Aquarium. I was stressed out because my mom gave Dan her critical eye assessment throughout the visit. Dan was quiet, and I wished there was more conversation, but it is hard to do when you are walking around an aquarium! Eventually, Dan and my dad got to know each other, and my mom made more of an effort. Dan was different from my unstable first husband, which was such a good different for me. Our relationship lacked drama which was so nice.

After we had been dating a while, Dan's father got in a car accident and was in the hospital. When Dan called to tell me this and canceled our date, I asked if I could go to the hospital with him. To my surprise, he said no. I headed to Sandy's house, had a few drinks, and complained about and questioned why Dan didn't want me to go with him to see his father. I felt vulnerable like I was not good enough, and maybe not that important to Dan.

I went home and sulked! Dan called, and I chose not to answer. Finally, I did answer, and Dan knew I was upset. He asked if we could go out for a drink. I agreed and tried to tell him why it upset me. He understood. While we drank, Dan pointed out a girl he had wanted to date in high school. She was pretty, and I was jealous immediately. My insecurities surfaced. He went to the bathroom and took forever to return. I figured he found the girl from high school and was talking to her while I sat there. When he returned, I was upset! My feelings for Dan made me insecure and afraid of being hurt. *Why would he want me of all people?* I thought he would probably dump me soon. Poor Dan didn't know what to do with me, but told me he had seen a guy from his past and couldn't get away from him. Ugh! My insecurities led me always to expect the worst. I was paranoid and conjured up thoughts that were not true. My poor self-esteem and jealousy stuck out like a sore thumb. A week later, Dan proposed to me! I was amazed and ecstatic and... accepted! I decided Dan did love me after all, and I could trust him. Dan was the first boyfriend who swept me off my feet like Bob had in my younger life. My parents were excited. They had had a chance to get to know Dan and liked him. A couple of days after we became engaged, Dan came to my condo with a beautiful ring that I adored!

MARRIAGE

Planning the wedding was fun, difficult, and stressful. My mom offered to make the bridesmaids dresses. Sandy, who was my maid of honor, was such a good seamstress so she made her dress. Dan and I had fun finding the church, the florist, photographer, DJ, and place for the reception. We did most of the planning as my mom and dad were three hours away. It was not like we were young kids getting married. Later, I discovered that my mom felt left out.

The day of my wedding, my mom gave me the silent treatment. This had not happened in a while. I overlooked it and tried to pull her into conversations. I was getting dressed, and I finally got fed up and upset with my mom's behavior. I slammed the door and sobbed in the bathroom.

Sandy told me later that my dad went to my mom and demanded, "You go and fix that!" I refused Sandy's knock, and then I heard my mom's voice. Reluctantly, I let her in. I had done my makeup, was in my dress, and the photographer was arriving any minute. My mom hugged me and apologized. She said her nose was out of joint because she had not been a part of the wedding planning.

I told her that it wasn't that I didn't want her to help, and reminded her that she had made two bridesmaid dresses. I explained that I hadn't wanted her to be stressed. Finally, I pulled myself together, although I looked like I had been crying. I was angry that mom had caused this and then acted as if all was fine.

We all jumped in the limo and went to the church. This was my day. My wedding. Dan's wedding. Our wedding. What a start to it! Dad stood next to me at the church and apologized for mom's behavior and told me how much he loved me. It was special to walk down the aisle with my dad, headed towards my future husband, Dan. They say you marry your father. Well, this time, I did. Dan is like my father in temperament and values. I finally got it right!

We went on a cruise for our honeymoon and had a wonderful time. I couldn't drink alone on the ship. I craved drinks but survived. We had fun, but by late afternoon, I wanted a drink regardless of what we were doing. There were times when what we were doing didn't include having a drink. It was not a live or die situation, but it was different not having a drink available. So, I hid my cravings. Our first year of our marriage, I became a "closet drinker." I drank when I got home from work and then stopped before Dan got home.

My behavior started to resemble my mom's. I gave Dan the silent treatment for some reason or other. Dan probably wondered if he made a major mistake marrying me. I conjured up things that I thought he was doing. I thought that his relationship with his co-worker was a threat to me, and I became jealous of every female in Dan's life. My insecurities caused me to sabotaged my marriage. I was testing whether he would stay or not. Talk about playing Russian roulette! Dan took courses at a local college. I would have had a couple of drinks while he was at class. When he came home, I would choose to not speak to him! It scared me because I was acting just like mom! I could not figure out why he would love me as I did not like nor love myself, so how could I understand someone else loving me?

I drank almost daily at home after work. I hid my stash of vodka and drank it with a diet soda. I didn't want to be a "regular," so I shopped at different liquor stores. I didn't hesitate to travel twenty-five minutes out of my way to get my alcohol supply. I was also blacking out, forgetting conversations I had had the night before with Dan. I didn't think I could cope without alcohol.

RECOGNIZING I NEEDED HELP

Dan and I were visiting my parents on the Cape, and my brother and his family were there. It was stressful to watch my mom be cold to my sister- in- law whom I adored. One morning around eleven o'clock I snuck some vodka into my cranberry juice with some ice. I snuck the vodka from my dad's supply.

I walked out onto the enclosed porch, and my brother asked: "Can I have a taste?"

I panicked and should have said, "No, I have a sore throat!" but I didn't think quickly enough and let him have my glass.

He took a sip and said, "Holy cow, what is in that?"

I smiled and walked away. My brother asked my parents and me if I had a drinking problem.

I said, "Definitely not."

My mom began watching me. I don't think Dan was around for this incident. Things died down at that point, but the seed was planted, and I wondered if I *did* have a problem. The fact that I hid my drinking from my husband didn't make me think there might be an issue?

In the second year of my marriage, I attended a

workshop on addiction. It is amazing how things in your life happen for a reason. It was a four-day workshop, and we were supposed to sign a contract promising that we would not drink for four days. I told myself, "fat chance," but signed the form. This was when it dawned on me that I might have a problem. I think I knew I had a problem and was getting closer to talking about it. I listened to the speaker and panicked. *What if this is true and I am an alcoholic?* I sought out the speaker who referred me to an addiction counselor.

I realized I could NOT stop drinking. It helped me function, or so I thought. *How in the world would I ever give this up? What would replace it?* I was at the stage of alcohol abuse, where on some days I had a drink ready to go for my trip home after work. I hid my alcohol consumption from Dan, or so I thought. My behavior was erratic. Dan never knew which wife would greet him when he returned home from work, the nice one, or the angry one.

After the workshop, I sobbed and told Dan that I thought I was an alcoholic, and I wanted an evaluation. He was kind and willing to help. My mom had told Dan my behavior was due to depression. In part, that was true, but the real reason was my addiction to alcohol. All I thought about was the women or men in the streets with the bottle wrapped in a paper bag.

I made an appointment to be evaluated and was diagnosed as an alcoholic. It was a lot to take in. I knew I was dependent on alcohol. I had been on antidepressants, but they could not work properly, because as I mentioned earlier, alcohol canceled their effectiveness. I was told I needed to work with a drug and alcohol counselor and might need an inpatient program. I did not want to go to a program where I would miss work, but I had missed work due to hangovers. I saw an alcohol abuse counselor but still drank.

I would wake up and tell myself, "I will not drink today," but when I got home from work, I drank.

I lied to Dan and told him that I had not been drinking when I was.

We had gotten a beautiful collie, that was my watchdog. "Hobbes" signaled me when Dan came down the hallway as I poured vodka into my glass of soda in the backroom from a closet. I swore each morning that I would not drink, but I could not stop. My drug and alcohol counselor suggested a rehab facility to get me started in my sobriety. I spoke to Dan, and we decided I should go to rehab. I was ashamed, but I shared the information with my principal at my school that I trusted. I told him I did not want others to know, and he agreed to keep it confidential. A couple of close friends knew I was going and they encouraged me.

The night before I left for rehab, I was petrified. I did not know what to expect and felt vulnerable. I drank alone that night. The rehab facility was about an hour away. When they checked me in, they went through all my belongings looking for any substances or sharp objects. They asked when I last had a drink, and I told them the truth.

I was ashamed, and the counselor said, "I would be surprised if you hadn't." That relieved me a little.

It was hard to say goodbye to Dan. They took me to my room, where I met my roommate. I hated having a roommate at first, but she was nice. I didn't speak much that first night and morning. I cried all night long and didn't get much sleep. I had emotions which shook me to my very core. *How had I gotten to this place in my life?* I was full of shame, guilt, and fear. I remember looking to the ground when I walked the halls.

I met some of the others there who were nice. We had a circle meeting every morning and evening where we went around and checked in about how we were doing in the program. We followed a schedule each day. The first day, I attended classes. I learned some valuable information such as, I had a disease, and I had not asked for it. I was allergic to alcohol because of my brain wiring. I had not realized this. They talked about feelings that we were all hiding from in some way, shape, or form. They told us we would need to deal with them eventually. This scared me. I knew that I did not like myself but did not know what I wanted or what I needed.

We met with a psychiatrist and had a physical. Our vitals were checked each morning when we woke up. The first week, my hands shook while I went through alcohol withdrawals. Some of the others had seizures during their withdrawals.

They gave me my antidepressants and thyroid medication each morning. At night, I would ask for aspirin for the headaches I had. I felt better by the end of the first week. Dan came to visit and brought Hobbes, and we went for a nice walk. It was good to see them both. I wanted to go back home with them but, knew I had more work to do. Dan was wonderful throughout my stay and we spoke often on the phone. I was so thankful for his steady, constant support.

Some of the nosier people in the condominium where we lived would ask Dan where I was while I was away. He just said I was fine and would walk away. Dan visited each weekend. It was always so hard to see him leave. I would share all I was learning and how I felt about things. Many husbands would have just left their wife at rehab, or left the marriage, period. I was and am so blessed.

In rehab they took us to recovery meetings off-campus. They were speaker - discussion meetings, and I was not yet ready to identify with other people's stories. I didn't quite understand the purpose of the meetings. It was a lot of information to take in each day.

As a side note, one day, while I was getting my meal in the cafeteria, I saw a familiar young person. She attended the school where I worked! We locked eyes. I smiled and got the hell out of there. I spoke to one of the people at my program and discovered that the adolescent group had been allowed to eat with the adults that day. They kept us separated after that. I was nervous, and I hoped she had learned about anonymity!

I enjoyed exercising during the day, but my back pain reared its ugly head. The alcohol had numbed my back. I learned a lot about the disease of alcoholism. I was surprised to find out that it is mostly genetic. To my knowledge, there were no alcoholics in my family. When I asked my parents, I found out my mom's father had been an alcoholic and had quit cold turkey before it became a major problem. His father had also been an alcoholic. There was the genetic tie. I inherited depression, anxiety, *and* the gene for alcoholism. Ugh!

Leaving rehab was good. I wanted to be home with Dan, but it was also scary. I knew that when I returned home, I needed to attend meetings, but I was not sure how they would help me. I needed to get a sponsor. I headed back to work after a three-week absence. I received a warm welcome. I met with one of the assistant principals and the principal. The assistant principal was angry; no one told him where I went. He could have prevented the students from our school going to the program where I was. I hated that he was upset and angry with me. The principal felt bad, but he had followed my wishes by not sharing with any of the other administrators where I had been. I wanted to keep my anonymity. It was not a great first day back.

A couple of weeks later, I saw the student I saw at rehab in the guidance office pointing at me and whispering to her friend. I glared at her, and that seemed to stop her in her tracks. My thought was *if you learned anything in rehab, it was anonymity!* I didn't see her anymore after that. I had felt safe in rehab. It was hard to go home and back to work and cope with feelings and pressures on my own and not drink. I began going to evening recovery meetings. I explained to a couple of women at one meeting, who asked me how I was doing, that I felt like a raw open wound. They completely understood my description. I was a lost soul.

I made it to four weeks of sobriety. In my recovery program, when a person is sober for one month, two months and on up to a year, they are recognized, which is very helpful and gives each person a boost to keep going. At the time, it did not mean much to me. I was obsessed with that thought that I could NEVER drink again. What a tall order. It was depressing. When we went to my husband's family gatherings, I found it difficult to watch others drink, knowing I couldn't. They had no idea I had gone to rehab or that I was an alcoholic. Dan protected me until and if I wanted to share this information with them. Years later, I shared it with members of Dan's family and they were and have been wonderful.

Dan stopped drinking to support me. I couldn't believe it and was so thankful. I thought it would be helpful in the beginning, but to this day, he still joins me in abstaining from alcoholic drinks. And, it still helps me.

I got a nice sponsor, but I did not understand the process or program, and did not ask. At about six weeks of sobriety, I don't remember what happened, but I stopped at the liquor store and bought a bottle of vodka. I had one sip of my diet soda and vodka, and found instant relief. They say when you stop drinking and then start back up, you end up right back where you were consumption wise, and it only gets worse. That is true. I went to a meeting and confessed I fell off the wagon. After the meeting, a woman said to me, "Wow, I would never confess if I took a drink. That takes guts."

This confused me. *So I wasn't supposed to be honest?* I received no support either. My first round with this recovery was not a positive one. No one reached out to me or showed me the ropes. However, I had not asked for help either. I had not reached my bottom because I went back to drinking for quite a few years. I had gone to rehab, not for myself, but to please others. My addiction to alcohol was not finished with me, yet.

I spoke to my parents, who suggested that maybe I could drink wine. That was all I needed to hear. Wine it was. I returned to having blackouts when I drank, and Dan was frustrated with me. I didn't remember the conversations we had. I repeated myself to him. If we made plans for the next day, I would repeat them to him while I drank and hoped that would drill it into my mind so that I would remember in the morning.

One day, I was walking down the hall at work with a friend, and she asked me, "What should I do if a friend smelled like alcohol in the morning?"

My response was, "Tell their supervisor." She was probably talking about me, and it made me think long and hard.

HITTING MY BOTTOM

Dan and I struggled with my drinking. I knew my drinking was worse, and it started to affect me differently. It wasn't working like it used to. My chaotic world was overwhelming and I had completely lost who I was. I couldn't tell you what would make me happy or what I really wanted to do. I was so miserable.

One day, we were walking with Hobbes around the condo complex, and I announced, "I can't do this anymore."

Dan looked at me, "Do you mean us?"

I responded with, "No, the drinking."

I was surprised he thought I meant us, but I certainly get it now. He never knew what to expect out of me, and perhaps, part of him wished I *did* mean us. I started going to the recovery meetings with a different purpose. I was still scared, but I knew I had to do something, or I would lose my marriage and maybe my job. I was miserable. I had definitely lost myself on so many levels.

I saw my psychiatrist who was glad I shared that I was an alcoholic with him. He gave me two weeks to find a sponsor. I needed this guidance because I was not seeing a counselor at the time (a psychiatrist prescribes medication and a counselor is who you can talk to on a weekly basis). I kept going to certain meetings I liked. My favorite was one on Sunday mornings. I heard a woman share her story, and I identified with her right away. She was older than me and seemed wise. I tried to find her after the meeting but couldn't. The next week I went back and found her. I asked her if she would sponsor me. She said yes! I went back to my psychiatrist with good news, just in time for my deadline. God puts people in your life when you need them.

The first thing my sponsor said to me was, "I will love you until you love yourself."

Her statement brought instant tears. *She would love me? I did not love myself. How could she say this; she didn't even know me?* But, her words were true. I agreed to call her daily on my way home from work. That was when I was most vulnerable to drink. I would stop by the liquor store on my way home if I didn't have a stash waiting for me. When I called, we would discuss how I was doing and what I was going to do when I arrived home. I had to have a plan. If I wanted to drink at any time of the day; I had to call her. This was so helpful, and the key factor was I *wanted* to get sober this time, for ME, not anyone else.

I attended women's recovery meetings with my sponsor, Kate. One meeting was on Friday nights. I was beat by Friday night, but I showed up. I learned that my sobriety had to take priority. I found women like me. The first Friday night I attended, I came face to face with a colleague, an advocate for students with whom I had worked. Then I saw a parent of one of my students! I freaked out and turned to Kate. I explained in a panic that I knew them, and she reminded me they were there for the same reason as I was. Ohhh! That made sense. I relaxed a bit and was thankful that anonymity was a recovery program's motto.

I listened and watched at meetings this time around. These women *laughed* at themselves and *smiled* a lot. It baffled me, and I wanted to be like them. I wanted what they had. I went to several types of meetings (which is how I could learn a different way to live my life). Most were women's meetings. I learned through Kate that women's meetings were easier because women could relate to one another. We could be more open about women's issues than we could at co-ed meetings. I finally found a place where I belonged! It might sound weird that I found recovery meetings with a bunch of alcoholics in recovery really wonderful, but it is so true. I was understood and they knew what I was going through.

At meetings, I heard people talk about surrendering to their disease. Admitting that I was powerless over alcohol was the first and most important step. Finally, I could admit this to myself and others. I knew if I took one drink, all bets were off. I would drink continuously if I took that first drink. People talked about taking sobriety one minute, hour, day, and month at a time. I found that when I wanted to drink if I waited a few minutes, the urge would pass. I had to fight that urge, busy myself, or call my sponsor. But, I could not stop the obsession yet.

SURRENDERING

I heard that once I surrendered to the disease of alcoholism and admitted my powerlessness over alcohol, I could look to a higher power to help me through difficult times. Some people used the group as their higher power. Some used God spelled backward: DOG. Or GOD meant a "group of drunks!" Anything that was beyond your power in the atmosphere could serve as a power greater than you.

My family attended the Presbyterian Church while I was growing up. Skating practices on Sunday mornings limited my time in church, but I prayed to God. Believing in a higher power was not hard for me. Unable to get rid of the obsession, my sponsor suggested that I ask God to remove it. I did this a couple of times, and all of a sudden, it lifted. No lie! The obsession to drink was gone. I really could not believe it. Yes, I still missed it, but that is quite different from an obsession. This was the beginning of my *spiritual* relationship with my higher power versus being *religious.*

I had drunk dreams early in sobriety. I would dream I got drunk and woke up in a panic. I was scared that I had had a drink! They were horrible, and I found out they were common. I hated them, but I was grateful they were only bad dreams, and I was able to wake up and

71

realize it wasn't real. Phew, crisis averted!

The first year was difficult. Facing the world without my security blanket was like walking into the unknown, naked, each day! This created anxiety. I was in daily contact with my sponsor. She taught me a valuable tool to use when I was upset. She had me think about whether the issue at hand would matter in a week, a month, or even a couple of days. She helped me realize that often I put my energy into matters that I had no control over, such as people, places, or things. I learned the serenity prayer said at each meeting.

Dan readily accepted my attendance at meetings and supported my recovery one hundred percent. I told him what Kate was suggesting and what we talked about when I was stressed out or was having a "crisis". Dan really grew to respect and like Kate.

The Serenity Prayer
God, grant me the serenity to accept the things I cannot change,
The courage to change the things I can,
And the Wisdom to know the Difference.

It goes on, but this is the abbreviated version. It has so much meaning, and I found myself saying it whenever I was stressed, whether I was at work or at home.

Dan and my family were proud of me as I continued to put weeks and months of sobriety under my belt. I educated my parents as much as I could. My brother and sister-in-law and nieces and nephews were supportive. It felt good. Gradually, Dan trusted that I wasn't going to drink. He was and is a major support for me. The cloudiness of my thoughts lifted, and I smiled more. I enjoyed my meetings and was so glad I had Kate by my side, walking me through the rough spots and problems.

At the end of my first year of sobriety, my back pain had increased to where I needed to seek medical assistance. It led to another surgery because I had more degenerated discs that needed to be fused. I was able to take pain medication responsibly at this point. I was nervous but determined to take it as prescribed. I could not jeopardize my sobriety. If I started abusing medication, I would have to start my recovery all over again, (You see, being addicted meant I could not safely use any kind of mind-altering substance). I did not want to do that. My recovery from surgery was long, and I still suffered from back pain. I went back to work as soon as possible, but the struggle with my back had just begun, as well as depression. The pain medication made me tired. I never had any euphoria from the medication, which I was so thankful for.

Kate had me work on the steps of my recovery program. As I worked through these steps, I learned how to manage my life in a much healthier way. I learned how to face my problems and deal with day to day living issues. It came time for me to list my resentments of people, places, and things. I had to write out a list of resentments of things or people who hurt or angered me. Also, the things I felt guilty about. I wrote down my role in these issues. *How did alcohol play a role in my behaviors?* I started by listing my mom and figure skating. As I wrote, I discovered how deeply both issues had hurt me and how angry I was. I had to list the wrongs I did and wrongs done to me. It was a time where I had to take a hard look at myself to discover where I made mistakes. I had to forgive myself for my mistakes and recognize my positive qualities. The task of finding the positive things about me got left out until my sponsor made me go back and list them. As with most alcoholics, I didn't focus on my positive qualities because of shame, guilt, and low self-esteem. As I grew, those feelings gradually lifted but I continue to have to work on this.

Next, I had to discuss all that I had written down with my sponsor. It is recommended we pick our sponsor or a trusted person such as a therapist, minister, or priest. It is important to find someone whom we trust and feel comfortable with. After all, we are revealing personal things that we would not tell just anyone. I rightly trusted my sponsor Kate. When I arrived at her house to bare my soul, I was nervous and scared. Kate made me feel comfortable and explained she would not judge me. I discussed my mom and how I never felt I could please her, how her behavior towards me affected me, even as an adult. I cried. The feelings I had were acknowledged and understood. It felt good to get out the feelings that I had held in for so long. I talked about the loss of figure skating and how deeply it saddened me. I had not known any other place where I belonged other than in a rink, skating. Once I included forgiving myself and listing my positive qualities, I learned I was a survivor. I had come through some difficult times and would survive future difficulties, but no longer needed to depend on alcohol to help me through.

We talked for about two and a half hours. I was drained. In conclusion, Kate told me to turn my resentments over to my higher power. She also told me to go home and burn my writings to signify that I was letting go of them. It was an amazing experience. I was heard with kindness and acceptance. My feelings were real, but they didn't have to haunt me anymore. I realized that I could forgive my mom for her behavior and that she had done the best she knew how raising me. I realized I mourned the loss of figure skating, but it couldn't go anywhere because I had never talked about it. Now, I could let go of it. I can think of figure skating and be thankful I had the opportunity to be a part of the sport. It gave and taught me so much that has helped me moving forward. It taught me to focus and reach goals, be determined when things get rough, to organize my time, and accept failure. I have learned to use my failures as learning experiences and to ask for help when I need it.

My dad always told me that as humans, we all make mistakes; it is how you react to the mistake that matters. He stressed to me that I should learn from my mistakes. When I drank, I made poor decisions, but I could not see it. Anything negative that happened to me while I was drinking was always everyone else's fault. I am not always a quick learner, and my need for control can make me repeat the same mistake several times before I learn what I need to change. Since doing these steps the first time, I have done a few more steps over again as different things that have popped up in my life. I will always go through this process when I find myself resentful.

My first Christmas sober was very hard. Dan suggested I call Kate. I was mourning the fact that the holidays meant parties I could not attend. I missed being able to drink socially. *Oh, wait a minute; I was never able to drink socially!* Harsh reality struck. I was taught not to look at "forever" when I thought about my drinking. Instead of thinking that I would never be able to drink again, I should only focus on the day at hand. That Christmas was hard, but I got through it with my husband and my sponsor. I attended a meeting that went on all day for those who struggled with sobriety and the holidays. It was good to be with people who could relate to my feelings.

My meetings were a place where I finally fit in. We all shared the isms of alcoholism (our character defects), and we all battled the disease of addiction. Often people who were addicted to pills, crack, or heroine attended our meetings as well. That was fine. We are all vulnerable to any type of mind-altering substance due to our disease of addiction. I met one woman who confessed that she was still smoking pot but was sober as far as alcohol. I spoke to Kate about it, as I didn't think she was kidding anyone but herself. She was not truly sober if she relied on something to take her mind away from reality. I felt bad for her because I knew she would have to face her demons.

Next, I was told to think about making amends to those I had hurt with my drinking. For me, that meant my family, and most importantly, my husband, Dan. It meant so much to me to make amends to Dan. I felt so badly for all I had put him through. I also made amends with friends that were affected in some way by my drinking. It felt good to make amends. Those whom I made amends to forgave me. That is not the case for everyone. And that is not what making amends is all about. It is up to me to make amends for those things where my drinking caused me to hurt someone in some way. I cannot however, control the outcome and others reactions.

HOSPITALIZATION

As I began my third year of sobriety, so many feelings that I had numbed myself to while drinking came bubbling to the surface and started to overwhelm me. I cried all the time, and my back pain started up again. I left early at the end of the school year to have another surgery where they fused the rest of my lumbar discs. This was another rough surgery. Screws and a cage were placed along my spinal cord to help support the fused discs. The doctor said I would be able to return to work at the beginning of the school year. I would have to wear a huge brace that created a big bulge under my clothes.

I was in pain, but went back to work. I was helping put together a program for Red Ribbon Week in October, which brings awareness to drug and alcohol abuse. We worked with some al-anon people who volunteered their help. I was overwhelmed with this task and tried to handle the flood of emotions. I felt like I was sinking and had no control over anything. I talked to my close friend, Lynn, who was also a counselor at the school and knew everything about me. She has been such good support and a great friend to me for many years! I remember one day waking up, and I was so upset and couldn't stop crying. I made an appointment with my psychiatrist, who saw me right away. I was suicidal. My doctor wanted to admit me to the psychiatric unit in the hospital. Part of this sounded good, but another part of it didn't. *What would work say? What would people think?* I said I would discuss it with Dan and get back to him.

I called Dan sobbing, and after a discussion, we agreed I should go into the hospital. My thoughts were all over the place. I was in this bottomless pit with no way out. I knew my husband had a gun in the house, and it was my plan to use it. I didn't even know where it was. I called my friend, Lynn, at school. She was relieved and told me she was proud of me for agreeing to be admitted and get help. She agreed to tell my boss. I also spoke to my sponsor, who was supportive and was glad I was getting the help I needed. I spoke to her daily while I was in the hospital and as soon as I got out. Once again, I felt ashamed. I also felt so badly that once again I was putting Dan through hell.

Incidentally, I found out that my boss proceeded to go to my office and announced in the outer office that I was in the "loony bin." I was angry about that, but knew he had his own issues. I lost any respect I had for him.

In the hospital, I cried and cried. My psychiatrist changed my medications, and I attended some groups. I was on a locked floor, which felt weird but also felt safe. I had a quiet roommate. We never connected, which was fine. I was there to feel better not to make new friends. One of my friends, who had worked at the high school in previous years, was now working in the psych unit. When I saw her, I was emotional and ashamed. I was embarrassed that as a counselor myself, here I was such a mess. She was kind and understanding, which made me even more emotional. I was a mess.

I was in the hospital for about five days and did better on my new meds. I was finally released to go home. Once again, Dan was by my side willing to help me any way he could. I don't know how he has remained with me all these years. Little did he know what he was in for when he married me. When I arrived home, I wanted to stay inside our house. I felt vulnerable, and was not prepared to face work yet.

My psychiatrist and I decided I was not ready to go back to work and that I needed to get into therapy. I spoke to my boss, and the head of the teacher's union, and they granted me a medical leave. They hired someone to fill my spot as a guidance counselor. I was grateful to have time to deal with my feelings and not have the pressure of work. I started therapy and continued my recovery meetings. The amazing part was that I did not think about picking up a drink through this ordeal. I knew that was not an option. There were more stuffed emotions, and they all came to the forefront. I could not hold them down anymore. I was a mess. But I was a SOBER mess. Never once while I was falling apart did I think a drink would help!

Shortly after leaving the hospital, I told my sponsor I wished I could go back to the hospital. When she asked, "why I felt that way", I told her " it was because I felt safe there." Each person's journey from addiction to sobriety can have difficult times. I had my husband, my family, close friends, and my friends in my recovery group to help me when I let them know what I needed. Asking for help and telling others honestly how I felt was still new to me and at first, made me feel helpless. I was fighting for my life, and I worked hard with my therapist, psychiatrist, and sponsor. I was feeling better each day. It felt good, but I was exhausted in dealing with all my emotions. I was learning how to change my self-talk, which was always putting me down. My self-confidence grew a bit, and I learned that I could speak up for myself, although it was scary in practice.

I was even worried that Dan was mad at me. If I didn't want to do something or didn't like something, I worried if I said something he would get mad at me. Dan had told me many times early in our marriage that it was okay to disagree with him and that if he got mad at me or I got mad at him, it was okay too. It didn't mean he didn't love me. I was middle-aged, and I was just learning about all this. I hated when people were mad at me, but was working on it. I was still a people pleaser but kept hearing at meetings, from my sponsor and Dan that I didn't need to apologize constantly for things that were not my responsibility. Man, so many bad habits from self-doubt and self-hatred to shake loose.

A couple of months later, I was contacted by the district office who informed me I either needed to resign or return to work in three weeks. I was caught off guard and not prepared for this ultimatum. I was not sure I was ready to return to work, but I didn't want to lose my job either. Dan was not home, and this woman acted as if she needed an answer right then.

I finally said, "Well, I guess I have to resign."

I had a therapy appointment right after that phone call. I told my therapist what happened, and he convinced me I was not making the best decision. We discussed whether I was ready, and he thought I was. I felt better as we spoke and decided I did not want to throw in the towel. When I got home, I called the district office to tell them I would be returning. When I reached the woman I originally had spoken to, she was EXTREMELY upset with me. She had in a matter of an hour and a half, done the paperwork to terminate me and had told my various bosses. After this all settled, I was rather angry with myself and with the woman. I felt bullied by her to make a fast decision, and I was mad at myself that I did not ask for time to make my decision. She could have told me that I had at least a day to get back to her with a decision. Following this incident, she had little time for me. I had made her job difficult and she had to undo all her wonderful paperwork.

In my recovery, I learned to release the feelings I had stuffed for so many years. I was no longer drinking them away. My new medication made my depression more manageable. I was relieved. Depression is not a fun place to be for anyone. There is help for depression. I had learned that if my medication doesn't work or stops working, I must let my doctor know. I don't have to suffer.

I returned to work, and the first day we had to give presentations. I still was not comfortable doing presentations. I hated being the focus of a large group! I was in a daze that day. I didn't know how I was holding it together and whether I would make it through the day. I said the serenity prayer almost every hour or half-hour. I felt like a deer in the headlights!

Gradually things fell into place at work. I disliked my job because I thought I was lousy at it. I had so much to work to do on myself, and I couldn't see how I could do a decent job. I liked the kids, but some days a few of their issues were too overwhelming.

I told my sponsor, and she asked, "Can you quit your job?"

My response was, "No."

I couldn't. We needed my salary to help pay for our house. It felt good to be out of the condo, and due to market increases, we finally made money selling our condo. We loved our house. I don't think buying a house would have been in the cards if I had not stopped drinking. If I had continued, I would have become sick and probably would have been divorced from Dan. I was grateful for my sobriety, even at this early stage.

Since I was sober, I thought my life would be easier than it had been in certain areas, such as work, but life does not work that way. I asked for help when things got rough and realized I didn't have to handle things on my own. I sat with my feelings about my job as I worked on my sobriety and focused on learning more about my disease and how it affected me emotionally, mentally, physically and spiritually.

My back gave me pain, especially when I was stressed, or when there was rain, snow, or I was tired. There was no way around taking pain medications to help control the pain so that I could work and live. I had restrictions on what I could and couldn't do. That frustrated me. I took my pain medication as prescribed. My primary care doctor was awesome and kept close tabs on me with my medication. Many people in recovery programs are against anyone taking medications like opioids! However, they do not always understand chronic pain. I know others who have similar pain issues who are also recovering alcoholics and who are responsible with their pain meds. I am upfront with my doctors about my alcoholism. There are several different opinions on this subject, but we all must make informed and careful decisions about it for ourselves. I will know if I am using my medication as an emotional crutch or not, and I must be honest with myself and others.

My fifth year of sobriety was a milestone. My program tells me to never forget where I came from. On my sobriety anniversary, I chaired a meeting and shared the story of my background, when I started drinking, and how I recovered. I benefitted from this as it reminded me of how far I had come. The most important part of giving my testimony was that maybe someone new or returning would hear something they could relate to that had the potential to help them and give them hope. I treasured having my sponsor give me my medallion each year. These medallions are significant to me and represent a lot.

I love my sponsor for all she has given me. She is a special friend. I do not think I would be sober today without her. She has been there through every trial and tribulation I have faced. Some people go through a couple of sponsors for various reasons. If someone has a sponsor who isn't working out, that is okay! If it doesn't work for whatever reason, they can be respectfully honest with their current sponsor, and find a new one. At times, sponsors will discontinue sponsoring a person if they feel they can go no further with a person or the person is not serious about getting sober.

I have been fortunate to have the same sponsor thus far. Thankfully she didn't fire me! Kate has helped me face some harsh realities. For example, when a friendship falls apart, and I want to save it, she has made me realize it isn't always my decision. I have a hard time letting go of things sometimes. Throughout my recovery, Kate has been honest with me. When she lets me have it, she does it with love. I know the difference. She doesn't put me down or shame me, she shares her wisdom with me, and it is a suggestion, not a command.

Her suggestions are usually right! Sometimes, I get stubborn and don't follow the suggestion at first. But eventually, I realize she is right. When I lost friendships, I felt it was my fault. Kate helped me realize that maybe I wasn't meant to have this person in my life forever. I would never think that way. I thought everything was always my fault. I still struggle with this concept; that it isn't always my fault. I need to look beyond this and decide if it is good for ME!! What a concept! And it isn't always about ME!!!

Finally, I started to feel self-worth and believe in and trust myself more. I began to love my job again, and I didn't run away from myself. I realized I had inner strength and something to offer others.

My program suggests that when someone starts drinking, they stop growing emotionally. Boy, was this ever true for me. When I stopped drinking, I was in my early twenties emotionally. I hated facing responsibilities because they terrified me. The little girl in me showed up and needed nurturing. When I was newly sober and didn't like my job, it was because I was still that twenty-year-old who was hurt and needy. The little girl in me never had a chance to feel whole and confident.

I began to enjoy my life, and decided I was where I should be, working with adolescents. I finally knew where I fit, as far as my career, helping kids. *How many years had this taken?* At least it happened! I thought outside the box to figure out ways to help students navigate high school and their emotions. I also enjoyed working with parents, for the most part, as well as with the staff. I had been doing this all along, but I finally enjoyed it. I loved watching my students grow. I think I always enjoyed it in my heart, but didn't trust myself enough to think that I was good enough.

My husband and I never had children, which is a sensitive subject for me. I would have been laid up the entire pregnancy due to my back problems. We could not afford this. I was in my late thirties when we got married, and so my age could have presented other medical issues as well. I was thankful I didn't have children with Don due to my depression and alcoholism, and a child would have kept me tied to my ex-husband. I was glad I didn't pass on these genes. But, I miss not having children. I loved my students very much, and some I loved like my own. I learned a lot from the kids I worked with every day. If I could help them in any small way, that made my day and job worth it. I brought work home with me in my mind because it was hard to turn my heart off after I saw and heard what some kids dealt with. Through experience, I learned to separate myself at the end of the day; however, sometimes in the evening or nighttime, I came up with some great ideas!

I shared more and more with certain people that I was a recovering alcoholic. When it came to students who were struggling with drug or alcohol abuse, I shared my background when I thought it might be helpful to them. Whenever I shared my addiction history, it was with the purpose to help them see that people can recover from their addictions. I was comfortable and grateful enough with my sobriety that I wanted to share hope with these kids. It is hard for adolescents to not participate in drugs or alcohol. Peer pressure is hard for some kids to fight. It is not for me to judge whether someone is addicted to either drugs or alcohol. That is for the individual and professionals to determine. When I had concerns I tried to lead these kids to our drug and alcohol counselor. But, the knowledge I had struggled with substance abuse made them feel more comfortable to talk to me about their issues.

I learned how to balance my life as best I could. I became a wife whose behavior was more even-keeled and sensible. I loved my mom despite how she raised me. I forgave her and realized that she did and does love me. I became a better sister, aunt, sister-in-law, you name it. It was because I wasn't altering my mind with alcohol anymore. I also learned to love myself and to be grateful for my life. I became closer to my higher power and learned to trust my gut when I made decisions. I learned I could make mistakes, and it didn't mean I am or was a bad person. I realized I didn't have to be perfect. What a relief!

Control was and is a major issue for me. Throughout the day, I turn my life over to my higher power and ask for guidance. In certain situations, I can't stop myself from trying to take that control back. When I try to control everything around me, I am in big trouble and it usually doesn't end well. Rather than holding back and waiting patiently for a situation to unfold before deciding, I ram my way into it and often make a mess!!
Wanting control is universal to alcoholics. We are not alone. When there is chaos, and I am frantic, I need to sit back, take a deep breath, and figure out what is going on with me. I think about what things I can control, within myself, and let go where I have no business being. In my recovery program, they say, you need to be responsible for your own stuff and not the other person's. That is, I need to let go of things I cannot control like people, places, and

things. I need to stick to my own business and not to others' unless I am asked. And if I say something that hurts someone, I need to take responsibility and apologize. But I have to be certain that I overstepped. By that I mean I am a recovering people pleaser as well. I can often fall into the habit of apologizing for things that are not my responsibility. So I need to think hard as to what I am truly responsible for.

Being in my head can be a dangerous place for me. Other recovering alcoholics can relate to this. I start listening to that negative inner voice telling me, "Oh you haven't heard from so and so because you said something that offended her," or "What did that person mean by her comment, was it meant negatively towards me?" This happens a lot when I isolate myself, and am not socializing at all with others. I must be careful not to get too comfortable being alone. My back doesn't allow me to participate in many social events I would like to, and as a result, I can get comfortable being alone. I have learned to recognize it, and when I do I make a call or get together with someone. Sometimes I go outside and take a walk.

Today I feel much more comfortable with who I am. I still have rough patches, but I have tools from my program that can help me through difficult times. What person doesn't have rough patches? I can call my husband who always has a calming effect on me along with a voice of reason, a friend, and my sponsor; seek out a counselor, etc., for help with sorting out my problems.

WHEN LIFE THROWS A CURVEBALL

When I reached ten years of sobriety, my world was rocked to its core. On my way home from a nighttime recovery meeting, I was approaching a two-lane intersection when I saw something coming out of the air and drop down in front of my car. I had no time to hit the brakes. At the last second, I realized it was a human being. The car to the left of me hit the girl while she was running across the road and was thrown in front of me. A group of girls were attempting to run across the street, not realizing that I, and the car next to me did not have a stoplight. I cannot tell you what ran through my mind other than panic and dread.

It was like an out-of-body experience. I was in a daze. I was taken by police car to the hospital for a blood test. I was numb. Dan could not be with me when they took my blood. The girl had been rushed to the hospital and I prayed she would be okay. It was all so hard to process. It is amazing how our bodies allow us to take in so much at a time knowing what we can and cannot handle. I was thankful that I was sober. I told the police I was returning home from a recovery meeting. The officer asked how many years of sobriety I had, and when I told him I had ten years, he congratulated me. They checked my phone to make sure I had not been on it and had been distracted. They released me to my husband at the hospital, and we drove home quietly. Dan was compassionate, per usual, but I could only imagine the thoughts running through his mind.

The following day, Dan heard on the news that the girl passed away. It felt like a punch in my stomach. They announced mine and the other's driver name. It was sinking in. I had killed a teenager. *How could this have happened? How was I ever going to live with this?* I don't remember talking to my sponsor, but I had. A good friend of mine, who was a secretary at work, called when she heard the news on tv. It was a brief call to let me know she was thinking of me. I realized I had better call my boss. I told them I would not be at work for a couple of days. The administration was kind, and I heard from others it was a tragic accident and it didn't sound like I had been in the wrong. I called my friend Lynn from school and asked her if she knew of any good lawyers. Her husband had been chief of police, and he recommended a good lawyer. I couldn't stop crying when I called my insurance company to explain what had happened.

One of my sisters' in-law, Mary, called me Monday morning and asked if she could come over. Dan had gone to work, and I was alone. I didn't think to ask him to stay home with me. So, Mary, who was also my good friend, came over and by that time my whole body was shaking. The accident continued to sink in little by little, and I was so thankful Mary was with me.

I spoke with a lawyer who took my case. I waited to find out if I would be found negligent/guilty in the accident and then if I was to be sued by the family. It was a scary time. My thoughts were incoherently racing. I was devastated for her family and friends. I couldn't help but think that it could have been one of my students, and I knew the student body would struggle for quite a while.

Through this whole ordeal, it never occurred to me to have a drink. My program was working in that I asked my higher power to help me get through this and to be with the victim's family and friends. I attended meetings, spoke to my sponsor daily, and was talking to Dan a lot as well. I was allowing others to help me and was not stuffing all my feelings. If I had stuffed my feelings I would have certainly been in jeopardy of drinking.

I was not charged at all in the accident, and neither was the other driver. I was relieved with this news but still had such a heavy heart. I returned to work and asked that coworkers not approach me to discuss the accident. This was a boundary I needed for myself. My coworkers were wonderful, and I received a lot of hugs and kind words which helped. The intersection where the accident occurred was one I drove by often. It was hard to drive after this. A few weeks later, I went by the intersection, and there were a cross and flowers on the corner. It broke my heart. I was constantly reliving the accident. I reminded myself that it was a tragic accident and that I had no control over it. My sponsor kept reminding me of this as well, and I was constantly asking for guidance from my higher power. I coped by talking about the accident so that I didn't stuff my feelings about it. It also helped to pray for the victim.

Three months after the accident, I received a formal document from the court requesting I show up for a deposition. The family was trying to sue the amusement company which had a fair going on across the street, the police, and the town for a faulty crossing signal. My insurance company hired a lawyer to go with me to the deposition. Dan and I met with the lawyer the day before my deposition. He explained how the process worked and advised me how to answer questions. He also brought out a letter the police had given him that had been sent anonymously to the police regarding me. It stated that this person knew I was actively drinking and using drugs and that they should thoroughly investigate me. I was shocked! *Who would do such a thing?* It was false, and I was devastated. *How could I prove it to anyone?* The only person who would know some of the information in the letter would have been from one of my n recovery meetings. The police could not follow up on it because it was not signed. That information was out there, and I had no way to defend myself. I knew it was a lie. I decided that for someone to outwardly try to hurt me who didn't even know me must be a very troubled person. I pushed this aside the next day because I had to appear for the deposition. The deposition was hard, I had to relive the accident, and they asked difficult questions. I was a mess afterward. The lawyer was there but couldn't say anything unless someone stepped out of line. The lawyer told me I had done okay, but I fell apart completely. As of this writing, it brings tears to my eyes. My heart goes out to anyone involved in an accident where there has been a fatality.

My sponsor and I suspected who might have written the letter. Her daughter had been a friend of the girl who passed away. She would often bring up the accident inappropriately in the meetings I attended. While we were not friends, nor did we speak to one another, I could tell she needed a lot of help. I needed to forgive her and try to move on, but it was a major challenge for me. I still get angry thinking about the hurtfulness of her action, but I don't want to judge her because I do not know what is going on in her life.

It has taken a long time to deal with this tragedy, and I still have guilt over this teenager's loss of life. Yes, it was a tragic accident, and I could not have done anything different other than not take that road home. Still, I contributed to that child's death. It will always be with me, but I have learned to forgive myself. I had to use my support system on an everyday basis. We all go through tragedy at some point in our lives. But with the help of others, we can make it through our difficult times. In my opinion, it can't be done alone. If I had tried to deal with my accident by myself, I might have started drinking again.

NEARING THE END OF MY CAREER

Over the years, my back got worse. I went to work, put a smile on my face, worked hard at my job, came home to do the bare necessities, and went to bed. My quality of life dwindled. I continued like this for quite a few years until I talked to my husband about retiring. I was beat. I had a hard time deciding what to do because I loved working with kids, but my back issues were taking over my life. I was sixty-one years old, and at sixty-two, I could retire and collect social security. We met with the state retirement bureau, and it seemed we could swing it financially. It was a difficult decision, but one I knew I needed to make. It was the right decision, but it was strange when I thought of leaving. People asked me if I was counting the days, and my response was NO! I wanted to do a good job and serve my students as well as I could. I worked hard getting schedules for the following school year squared away, and recommendations written. I wanted to leave my job feeling like I gave it my all until the end. It was hard saying goodbye to the kids, staff, and parents.

Before the end of the school year, I had a spinal stimulator put in to help with my pain. The initial trial gave me good results, but once I had surgery to put the stimulator in, it did not create the same results! I wondered if I had made a mistake. In May, I was admitted to the hospital because of pneumonia. I became septic as well, so it was serious. My heart rate was low, so I was on the cardiac floor, where they could monitor my heart. My final year at my job was a roller coaster! It was the right decision, although not the one I wanted. I would have liked to stay at my job for a few more years, but my health had to come first.

Once in retirement, I missed working with the kids terribly. I missed the structure of my days and felt lost. I applied for a part-time job at an animal hospital. However, my back prevented me from being able to handle the job, so I had to quit. I then decided to sub at the high school. Substitute teaching helped me to have some contact with the students and the staff. At one point I was a temporary office assistant sub at the school counseling office for two and a half months. My former boss made it possible for me to work mornings, but it was still a strain on my back. I fulfilled the tasks requested of me and realized I could not do it again.

Also, in my first year of retirement, our beloved collie, Bailey, needed to be put to sleep. His back and hips were bad, and we had to consider his quality of life. It was so sad. While we had been through this before with our previous collie, Bailey was my "sober" dog. He had only known me sober. I thought I could finally spend time with him now that I was retired, but it was not meant to be. That day was horrible. It was the first time I saw Dan cry. It is a lousy thing to have to play God, even though we knew we were doing the right thing for our dog. Dan didn't want another dog due to his allergies, so I decided to try living without a dog to respect his wishes. Living without a dog was a tall order.

THE LOSS OF MY DAD

About two or three years before I retired, my parents moved to assisted living in a nearby town. My Dad previously had some dementia but once in assisted living it became worse. The year before I retired, he was moved to the memory care locked unit where he could receive better care. When I would visit, sometimes he remembered who I was, and sometimes he didn't, but he always smiled. He started sleeping more and more in his lazy boy chair.

One day, during my first year of retirement, I found him in his bed, which was unusual. The nursing staff said he was not doing well. They informed me he would need to go to the hospital. My mom did not want him going to the hospital, and I didn't want that either. They suggested we bring in Hospice. I knew this wasn't good, but they said it might only be needed temporarily, and that he would get better. However, things got worse fast. That night, I got a call from Hospice, saying my dad could pass away very soon.

My brother planned to fly out the following day. But the next day, when I went to see dad and sit with him again, I had a feeling that was it. I spoke to him and could tell he knew I was there. A minister came in and said the

Lord's Prayer, and my dad started trying to say it, too! I said it along with them. After the minister left, my dad's breathing changed. I got the nurse and I told dad we were all with him, and that it was okay. He took his last breath and passed away. My mom came in right as he passed away. She was there to give him a final kiss on his forehead. I was devastated. I had such mixed emotions. I was glad he was not in pain anymore and was with God, but I was also sad to have to say goodbye.

I had to take charge as my mom didn't know what needed to be done. I spoke to my brother again and shared the horrible news. I felt so bad for him that he could not be there with dad before and when he passed away. I knew that was so hard for him.

If I had still been drinking, I would not have been present enough to do the things mom needed me to. I also would not have been there while my dad was dying. Sober, I was able to feel my pain but also step up and handle things that needed to be done. I adored my dad and hated losing him. I ached inside, yet was able to put one foot in front of the other, knowing I was not alone. I had to find a place to have my dad cremated and then arrange for his burial at the state military cemetery. I would not have been there to support my mom the way I needed to be if I hadn't been sober. I contacted my sponsor to let her know and spoke with her that evening. I asked my higher power to take good care of my dad and to help our family through our grief.

We had known ahead of time we would bury my parents at the state military cemetery, which was about forty minutes away. We asked the minister at the church I attended to speak at the funeral. One of my brother's daughters, Brittany, wrote a special poem about her grandfather, and it brought us joy and tears. It completely captured his essence. I still have the poem and will always cherish it. My mom could not make the services because she was too distraught. This was hard for my brother and me, but we knew we had to move forward without her. The minister read my niece's poem, and it helped those who attended who didn't know my dad to understand who he was. I was blown away by some of the people who showed up from my former job. Never did I imagine them making the trip to pay their respects.

The sun shone brightly into the chapel at the cemetery surrounded by a snow-covered cemetery on a cold and windy day. During the brief ceremony in the Chapel, we looked out a huge picture window where a Navy man in uniform appeared outside as the wind swirled the snow around him, and played Taps. This was beautiful and emotional for all. They gave the flag to me, and I gave it to my mom. My cousins on my dad's side drove in from New York, and after the ceremony, we went out to a favorite restaurant of my dad's. My brother and I were exhausted, but it was so nice to be with my dad's family. Dan was so sad at the loss of my dad as well. He was very fond of my dad and it was certainly a mutual feeling.

I still miss my dad! I have many happy memories that I keep in my heart and soul. I am thankful that my dad saw me get sober and living a life that was not full of drama. I also knew he was proud of me as an educator, and that felt good. He was certainly the best dad I could have ever had. I am grateful to him for the many things he taught me and showed me through example.

Before my dad passed away, we had to find another assisted living facility for my mom as her long-term care insurance was running out, and she could not afford to stay where she was. I visited several places and finally found one that was affordable and closer to Dan and me. Unfortunately, we were supposed to move mom shortly after my dad passed away. The move was difficult for her. Thankfully, she had a person from hospice visiting her to help her with my dad's death. Understandably, she was a bear to me during this move. But it was hard to ignore the harsh comments. I knew she had lost her husband, had to adjust to a new place to live, and cope with all her feelings. But I also needed to watch out for myself and give myself time to grieve.

I love my mom even though she can push my buttons. There are times when I need to walk away from her, which I would never have done in the past. That is growth. The little girl in me still needs her approval, and I have to deal with that. I know mom is proud of me, and I know she loves me. These are things that before, and while I drank, I did not know. Can she still hurt me? Of course. But I am learning that I allow myself to be hurt by her. I have tools today, thanks to my sobriety program that can help me deal with her.

When my mom is argumentative, I let her know I need to leave as things will get worse.

This upsets her, and she will say, "Oh sure, just leave, don't deal with it,"

My response, "I love you mom, bye, bye." If I were drinking, the fight would be horrendous, and I would say things I would not remember or regret. Nothing would get resolved. By walking away, the argument dies out, and we move onto the next day. Do I always walk away and avoid a fight? No! But I am working hard on this because I realize it isn't going to end well for either of us if I don't. It is called establishing boundaries, which I never knew I needed or I deserved! By telling someone I am not going to listen to their negative/angry words and walking away, I am saving myself from saying things I will regret and doing the same for them. When I allow myself to say "no" to something I don't want to do, I again am setting a boundary for myself. Establishing boundaries is a work in progress for me. I have to continually work at not people pleasing, which gives others the message that they don't have to respect my feelings. And I am the one who allows it to happen unless I establish those boundaries.

RUFUS

After my dad passed away, I continued to try to live without a dog. I was still lonely from the loss of Bailey. It wasn't good for me to be home alone and I missed the companionship of a dog. As the months passed, I became angry that I couldn't get a dog. Each time I tried to bring it up, Dan was still against it.

Finally, I told Dan we needed to talk. I took a walk first to help me to process what I was feeling and how to say it without anger. When we talked I explained that I had tried to fulfill his wishes, but I was home alone a lot while he was busy working. I told him I couldn't do it anymore and needed a dog. I told him I would take full responsibility for him. His response surprised me as he told me he expected this conversation. He actually had looked for puppies back in the winter. He asked me what kind of dog I wanted. I offered to look at hypoallergenic dogs, but he wasn't interested in those breeds. I told him it was his choice and he picked a Collie again. Instantly, I looked online for breeders in our area. If I had not been sober, I would have had a drink the minute Dan told me he didn't want a dog. I would not have tried to fulfill his wishes, and would have been very self-centered about it and created chaos. I learned how to voice my thoughts and needs rather than stuffing them and feeling they do not matter, all the while building a resentment.

I found a breeder with a twelve-week-old puppy. We planned to visit her the following weekend. We saw him, fell in love at first site, and bought him right away. What a handsome boy he was and is. We batted around names. Dan came up with "Rufus," and I came up with "Murphy." When we got him home, we decided he was a "Rufus."

Rufus has turned out to be our special needs dog. He was frightened of strangers and scared of new things at first. If you brought in a bag and placed it on the counter, he barked and ran away. Rufus has improved a great deal. We have worked with him, and he is on medication, which helps with his anxiety. We love him dearly, and I am grateful I have the time to be with him and work with him. If I still drank, I would not have handled Rufus' behavior well. I would have been impatient and would not have figured out ways to help him. The focus would have been on me and my needs.

I was fortunate to have met a person who became a good friend who also has a tri-color female collie who comes over to play with Rufus. They have the BEST time. I am also able to visit the breeder with Rufus, and we take great walks in the woods with his tribe. In recovery, I can find peace, such as having a dog as a companion who I can enjoy sitting outside with and listening to the birds. When I was an active drinker, I didn't know this kind of peace, at all! I did not focus on things that make me happy like nature, animals, and friends. I only thought about if I had enough alcohol to get me through the next night.

WORKING ON ME

Getting into a recovery program is not just about recovering from your addiction, but also recovering the person you were meant to be. It isn't just about stopping the substance. It is also about healing the inside where things have been stuffed and avoided for too long.

Ego and self-centeredness are discussed a lot in my recovery program. This has been a hard area for me to grasp. Some people's egos are right out there and outspoken, but this wasn't me. I learned that fear is self-centeredness. When I think about it, when I am scared, I am thinking of myself. As my sponsor told me recently, some self-centeredness is good. For instance, when we are in a bad situation, we get scared, and we MUST think of ourselves for protection. When we stop thinking of our own issues all the time, we can reach out to others, listen to our higher power, and live a calmer life. When my mom pushes my buttons, I become angry, and an automatic fear comes to the surface. By making it about me I am allowing her to control me. But when I realize it is not about me but instead about her and her fears I can react so much differently. I have also learned to walk away when things are not going to end well. Refusing to engage in a fight is a healthy reaction.

When things scare me in general, I am thinking of myself and am shutting down to the new possibilities that might be available to me. It is stepping outside the box. The box is me, whom I try to protect, and I can, at times, get in my own way.

Another important lesson I learned is that I cannot control others or change others! I can only change myself. It is up to me to figure out what is going on inside me at any given moment, and then figure out from there what I need to do.

I believe that life and bad situations happen to us all. I don't believe that a higher being creates these bad situations. I do believe, however, that I have a higher power that is there to guide me through any situation. When I stop trying to control every little thing around me and relax and see where it will lead, I can make better decisions about what to do (or not do) next. This is a lifelong lesson for me. As I mentioned, I try to take the controls back. I am not the most patient person when it comes to my own life. So, I must step back and push myself to let things be and not feel that I must solve every issue that comes along right away. I need to *pause* and let things unfold as they are meant to. The situations will resolve, maybe not the way I want but it is how it is supposed to be.

My relationship with my mom can be erratic. What I am realizing and learning is that it isn't about me. It is my mom's fears and insecurities that drive her to lash out at me and others who are responsible for her care. It is up to me to not own her hurtful comments and behaviors. This makes so much sense in my head. In my heart, it is a daily battle to keep it real and not take on her "stuff." I am not always good at handling it, but I keep in touch with my sponsor, voice my feelings at my meetings, and ask my higher power for help. Overall, I am glad I can be available to help her. Again, if I drank, it would not be possible. Because I am sober, I can try to give back to her all that she gave to me, which includes so much, in a good and loving way.

I am still and will probably forever continue to deal with my back. This frustrates me. I don't like it at all when my ability to do things I enjoy is not possible due to the pain I have. I get resentful and can get depressed. My initial reaction when I get depressed or frustrated is to turn within. Eventually, I get angry enough that I reach out for help. Just because I am sober, doesn't mean my life is all roses and sunshine. But I do know that if I were to pick up a drink, I would not just be hurting myself and all I have worked for and accomplished; I would be hurting those around me whom I love so much, as well. I like having a clear mind. I don't ever want to go back to the craziness that surrounded me when I drank. And I NEVER want to forget where I came from.

The disease of addiction gives us a lot to work through. If we are honest with ourselves and others, and realize when we need to pay attention to things such as our health, (physically, emotionally, and spiritually) we will learn and grow from our situations. When we work on our recovery, we must pay attention to our body, mind, and soul. All these areas are affected by the disease of addiction.

"Remaining the right size" is important, and has been spoken about in my recovery groups. This means being humble. I try not to let my ego think I am better than the next person and realize we all have gifts as well as flaws. I hope people will forgive me for my flaws, and I must do the same for others. Do I judge others or compare myself to them? Yes. But at least I can catch myself now when it happens, and continue to work on it. When I judge others or compare myself it is from fear. What others look like or act like is none of my business. If

I am right sized, I look at others for their positive attributes. But I am not perfect by any means.

I call it *coming clean* with my addiction and taking responsibility for my feelings and behaviors. As an addict, I need to keep an open mind and always be willing to learn about myself so that I can continue to grow and continue to live a clean and sober life. The healing process can be difficult but so, so worth it. It is also a wonderful thing if I can help another who is beginning their journey through recovery, no matter what their addiction.

The End

EPILOGUE

If you have a substance abuse problem, please know you can get better. I NEVER thought I could lose my security blanket of alcohol. But I can tell you that through hard work, perseverance, and listening, you can live a sober life. I am living proof. I wish everyone could have a program for life like I do, whether addicted or not. Some people do have a program through their religious practices. I learned that the scars of my past don't have to rule my life or own me. Yes, I can get stuck in my muck, but I have a choice as to whether I want to stay there or not. I have choices today that I didn't have when I drank. My world was small and scary while I drank. Now it is open and full of opportunities when I allow myself to see and experience them.

I will be the first to admit it is hard to break a pattern that I became secure with and give up a substance that I thought helped me. But remember, I did NOT do it ALONE! I had a lot of support from so many. Now, whenever life brings me down, I have people I can turn to and a program I can follow. I have learned a new way of living life, which is much healthier. I finally found my voice. I can tell people what I need, what I want, and whether I agree or disagree. It is still hard sticking up for myself at times; I am learning. My life is a learning process every day. And I love the saying, "God isn't finished with me yet." I am a continuous work in progress, and continue to learn about myself and others each day as long as I keep an open heart and mind. I have finally realized I don't have to be perfect. That is exhausting! No one can be perfect. We can only be human and try to do our best.

Made in the
USA
Middletown, DE